I0625785

THE COZY APOCALYPSE

Finding Joy When Everything's on Fire

QR McKinsey

Copyright Page

© 2025 QR McKinsey | All rights reserved

No part of this publication may be reproduced, distributed, or transmitted in any form or by any means without the prior written permission of the publisher, except in brief quotations for critical reviews and certain other noncommercial uses permitted by copyright law.

But seriously—if you're screenshotting passages to send to a friend while sipping wine in your bathtub during a rolling blackout, you're good. The world is burning. Share the blanket.

For permission requests beyond what's legally allowed, write to:

Half-Ass Revolution Press

📭 hello@halfassrevolution.com

🌐 www.halfassrevolution.com

First Edition: June 2025
ISBN: 979-8-9991388-0-4

IMPORTANT DISCLAIMER:
This book is a cozy bunker for your brain, not professional advice. The author is not a licensed therapist—just someone who knows how to laugh while reading disaster headlines and folding laundry. If you need actual clinical guidance, please talk

to a professional with credentials and a coffee mug that says "Feelings First." The author assumes zero responsibility if you stop over-functioning and someone else finally learns how to find the damn scissors.

Published by:
Half-Ass Revolution Press
A division of Strategic Absence Media Group
"Revolutionizing life, one half-assed effort at a time"

Book Design by: Perfectly Adequate Designs
Cover Illustration by: Cozy Chaos Studios
Edited by: The "Emotionally Stable Adjacent" Editorial Team

Printed in the United States of America—on paper that's probably about to get splashed with espresso, toddler tears, or existential dread. Possibly all three.

ACKNOWLEDGMENTS

This book exists because I needed it first. But it became what it is because of the people who helped me figure out how to live through these absolutely bonkers times without losing my mind—or my sense of humor.

To my daughters, who remind me daily that the apocalypse is no excuse for not making snacks or finding reasons to dance in the kitchen. You are my best teachers in the art of finding joy in ordinary moments, even when the news makes me want to hide under a blanket forever. Thank you for your patience during the writing process and for your expert consulting on whether my jokes are actually funny.

To the parents in my orbit who are also trying to make dinner while doomscrolling—this book is as much yours as mine. Thank you for the late-night texts, the grocery store therapy sessions, and for normalizing the fact that sometimes "thriving" looks like everyone being fed and nobody crying (including the adults).

To my fellow indie authors who shared wisdom about everything from cover design to marketing without making me feel like an imposter. The generosity of this community never stops surprising me.

To the readers of Half-Ass Revolution content who've been encouraging me to write about these themes. Your messages about finding permission to be imperfect while still caring deeply about the world gave me courage to tackle this project.

To the researchers, journalists, and thinkers whose work on resilience, climate psychology, and collective care informed these pages—especially those studying how humans actually survive difficult times rather than how they should theoretically survive them.

To my local coffee shop, which provided both caffeine and the kind of background noise that makes writing possible. And to my houseplants, who served as silent writing companions and occasional sources of procrastination.

To everyone who's trying to create moments of beauty and connection while also staying informed about genuinely concerning global trends—you get it. This weird balancing act we're all doing matters, and your efforts to stay human during inhuman times inspire me daily.

And finally, to anyone reading this book while something is burning (literally or metaphorically) in the background—thank you for taking time to consider that maybe, just maybe, finding joy isn't giving up on the world but giving ourselves the energy to keep engaging with it.

The world is still burning. But we're still here, figuring it out together, one cozy moment at a time.

CONTENTS

INTRODUCTION: The World Is Burning (But Your Hair Looks Great)

Let's start with the obvious: everything is a goddamn mess.

The planet is melting. Democracy is crumbling. Your phone just notified you about another impending disaster while you were trying to enjoy your coffee. Your social media feed is a hellscape of takes so hot they could power a small city. Your anxiety is at an all-time high, and somehow, inexplicably, you're still expected to make dinner and fold the laundry and be a functioning human.

Welcome to The Cozy Apocalypse. Population: all of us.

I'm not here to tell you things aren't that bad. They are. I'm not here to offer inspirational platitudes about how everything happens for a reason. It doesn't. And I'm definitely not here to suggest that if you just manifest harder or practice more gratitude or drink more water, all the world's problems will suddenly become manageable.

What I am here to tell you is this: You can acknowledge that everything is falling apart AND still find moments of ridiculous joy. You can be terrified about the future AND laugh until you snort wine through your nose. You can feel utterly overwhelmed AND create pockets of peace that make life not just bearable, but occasionally beautiful.

This isn't toxic positivity. This is survival.

This book was born from a simple observation: we're all trying to navigate the apocalypse (pick your favorite flavor—climate, political, economic, technological) while simultaneously attempting to live our normal, messy human lives. We're doom-scrolling through news of environmental collapse while waiting for pasta water to boil. We're having existential crises in the Target checkout line. We're contemplating the collapse of civilization while getting a root canal.

It's absurd. It's overwhelming. And somehow, we keep going.

I wrote this book because I needed it. Because I found myself paralyzed by the sheer magnitude of *everything*, unable to reconcile my deep worry about the state of the world with my equally deep desire to enjoy my limited time on this burning planet. I wrote it because I was tired of being told to either panic completely or ignore reality entirely.

There had to be a middle path—a way to face harsh truths while still finding reasons to get out of bed in the morning (besides, you know, the screaming alarm and responsibilities).

In these pages, you won't find:

- Instructions to "just think positive!"
- Suggestions that your anxiety is unreasonable
- Demands that you save the world through individual action
- Judgment for your coping mechanisms (well, most of them)
- The expectation that you'll emerge as some enlightened disaster guru

Instead, you'll find:

- Permission to acknowledge that things are genuinely difficult
- Practical strategies for creating moments of peace amid chaos
- Scientific research on resilience that doesn't make you want to punch a wall
- Stories from fellow disaster-navigators who are figuring it out as they go
- Ways to find meaning and even joy without denying reality

- Validation that sometimes just keeping yourself alive is achievement enough

This book is organized into five parts, moving from acceptance of our current reality to practical strategies for building resilience, finding joy, developing useful skills, and connecting with the bigger picture. You can read it straight through or jump to whatever section feels most necessary in your particular apocalypse moment.

Throughout these pages, I'll share research, stories, and strategies, but always with the understanding that your mileage may vary. What works for one person's nervous system won't work for another's. What feels meaningful to me might feel pointless to you. The goal isn't to follow some perfect apocalypse-navigation protocol but to create your own personalized approach to finding joy amid destruction.

Because here's the truth: the ability to find moments of peace, connection, and even delight while acknowledging the very real problems we face isn't frivolous—it's necessary. It's what keeps us human. It's what gives us the energy to keep going, to help others, to maybe even work toward solutions. Joy isn't the opposite of awareness; it's the companion that makes awareness bearable.

So pour yourself whatever gets you through (coffee, wine, adaptogenic mushroom elixir—no judgment here), get comfortable, and let's talk about how to build a cozy little life while the world burns around us. Not because we're ignoring the flames, but because we've accepted them as part of the landscape—and decided to live anyway.

After all, the apocalypse is here. We might as well make it cozy.

CHAPTER 1: Yes, Everything Is Actually That Bad

The Validation Chapter: Why Toxic Positivity Can Go Fuck Itself

The first time I realized toxic positivity was poisoning my life was at a baby shower. My friend Sarah had just lost her job, her marriage was on the rocks, and she was dealing with chronic pain that her doctors kept dismissing. When someone asked how she was doing, she admitted things were rough.

The response? "Just think positive! It could be worse!"

I watched Sarah's face fall, then rearrange itself into that strained smile we all know too well. The one that says, "I'm dying inside but I'll pretend your useless advice just changed my life."

That's when I wanted to flip the miniature quiche table.

Let's be crystal clear about something: telling people to "just stay positive" when they're drowning is not helping. It's emotional gaslighting. It's the equivalent of telling someone with a broken leg to just walk it off. It's bullshit.

And we've all been drowning lately.

Every day brings a fresh batch of crises. Climate disasters. Political meltdowns. Economic uncertainty. Health threats. And that's just the collective stuff, not counting your personal catastrophes—the sick parent, the struggling child, the job that's sucking your soul dry, the relationship that's more exhausting than enriching.

When someone looks at this absolute tsunami of legitimate problems and says, "Just focus on the good stuff!" what they're really saying is: "Your negative feelings make me uncomfortable, so please hide them."

What we need isn't more forced smiles. What we need is validation.

The Relief of Admitting Things Are Terrible

There's a unique kind of relief that comes with saying, "This is awful," and having someone respond, "Yes, it absolutely is." Not "Look on the bright side," not "At least you have..." Just simple recognition that your experience is real.

Research from Harvard psychologist Susan David shows that acknowledging difficult emotions— rather than pushing them away—is actually associated with better psychological health and resilience. When we validate our own suffering instead of shaming ourselves for it, we create space to actually process what's happening.

Think about it: have you ever had a problem that was fixed by someone telling you to "be more positive"? Has anyone ever "good vibes only"-ed their way out of a genuine crisis? Of course not. But I bet you've felt the weight lift, even momentarily, when someone simply acknowledges: "That sounds really hard."

So here it is, your official permission slip:

Things are hard right now. Probably harder than they've been in your lifetime. You're not imagining it. You're not overreacting. You're not "too sensitive." Your anxiety about *gestures vaguely at everything* is not irrational.

We're living through multiple overlapping crises, and it's exhausting. The constant background hum of dread isn't a personal failing—it's a reasonable response to unreasonable circumstances.

And admitting that doesn't make you negative. It makes you honest.

Why Your Anxiety Isn't Wrong (It's Just Exhausting)

Let's talk about that anxiety for a minute. The 3 a.m. ceiling-staring. The doom-scrolling you can't seem to stop. The way your chest tightens when you hear yet another news alert.

Your brain isn't malfunctioning. It's doing exactly what it evolved to do: scan for threats and prepare you to respond. The problem is that our Stone Age alert systems were designed for immediate physical dangers—a predator, a rival tribe, a poisonous plant—not for endless, abstract, global threats we can do very little about individually.

Our ancestors faced acute stress: run from the tiger, fight the enemy, survive the storm. Then rest. Their bodies got to complete the stress cycle. But we're stuck in chronic stress: constant exposure to threats we can see but can't directly fight or flee from. Our nervous systems never get the all-clear signal.

Neuroscientist Robert Sapolsky calls this "psychological stress," and it's particularly damaging because:

1. We can stress about things that haven't even happened yet
2. We can stress about things that will never happen
3. We can stress about things we can't control
4. We can stress about the fact that we're stressing

It's like your internal fire alarm is constantly blaring, but you can't find the fire, can't put it out, and aren't allowed to leave the building.

No wonder you're tired.

And no wonder conventional anxiety advice often feels so inadequate. "Just breathe" isn't super helpful when the air itself seems toxic. "Stay in the present moment" is cold comfort when the present moment is precisely what's freaking you out.

What's worse, we've created a culture that treats anxiety as a personal failure rather than a reasonable response to unreasonable circumstances. We're told to meditate, exercise, journal, hydrate, and therapy our way out of feelings that are actually appropriate reactions to a world gone mad.

Don't get me wrong—all those coping tools have value. We'll talk about them later. But first, we need to stop pathologizing our discomfort. Sometimes anxiety isn't a disorder. Sometimes it's a messenger telling us something is wrong—not just in our heads, but in our world.

The Problem With "It's All In Your Head"

"It's all in your head" might be the most dismissive phrase in the English language. It implies that if you just thought differently, you wouldn't be suffering. It places the burden of change entirely on you, not on the circumstances causing your distress.

But here's the inconvenient truth: many of our problems aren't just in our heads. They're in our systems. They're in our institutions. They're in our environment.

Climate anxiety isn't just catastrophizing—the planet really is warming at an alarming rate. Political stress isn't just partisanship—fundamental rights really are under threat. Economic worry isn't just scarcity mindset—wealth inequality really has reached staggering levels.

These are external realities, not cognitive distortions.

When we frame legitimate concerns as merely psychological problems to be fixed, we:

1. Shame people for appropriate emotional responses
2. Discourage collective action by individualizing systemic problems
3. Waste energy trying to adjust to circumstances that actually need changing

This doesn't mean we're helpless. It doesn't mean we should wallow. It means we need to be honest about what's personal (our reaction) and what's structural (the situation we're reacting to).

Finding Clarity Through Honesty

There's a strange paradox at work here: acknowledging how bad things are can actually help us feel better.

When we stop pretending, stop forcing positivity, stop minimizing real problems, we liberate energy that can be used for actual coping. We can direct our attention toward what truly matters rather than exhausting ourselves with emotional theater.

This isn't about surrendering to despair. It's about standing in truth. It's about creating a solid foundation of reality from which to build resilience.

Think of it like this: if you're trying to navigate out of a forest, the first step isn't positive thinking—it's accurately assessing where you are. Pretending you're not lost when you are just guarantees you'll wander in circles.

So take a moment right now to be honest with yourself about what's hard. Not to wallow, not to complain, just to acknowledge. Maybe write it down. Maybe say it out loud. Maybe just sit with it quietly.

"This is hard. This hurts. This scares me."

Feel the peculiar relief that comes with dropping the pretense.

Now you're ready for the next step—not denying the darkness, but learning to build a fire within it.

Because here's the truth: accepting that things are bad doesn't mean giving up on good. Quite the opposite. It means you can stop wasting energy on denial and start directing it toward what actually helps. It means you can be strategic rather than delusional. It means you can find authentic joy rather than manufactured positivity.

In the chapters ahead, we'll explore exactly how to do that. But first, we needed to clear away the toxic positivity that keeps us stuck in fake smiles and real suffering.

The world is burning. That's not your fault. And you don't have to pretend it isn't happening to prove you're resilient.

True resilience starts with truth.

CHAPTER 2: Your Disaster Is Not a Competition

Why Comparing Trauma Is Pointless (And We All Do It Anyway)

Have you ever caught yourself thinking something like this?

"I shouldn't be upset about my problems when people are literally losing their homes to wildfires."

"Other parents have it so much worse. At least my kid is healthy—I have no right to complain about being exhausted."

"People survived world wars and the Great Depression. This is nothing compared to that."

We've all done it. The mental gymnastics of comparing our suffering to others' and deciding we don't deserve to feel bad because someone, somewhere has it worse. As if pain were a finite resource that should be distributed only to the most deserving.

I call this the "Suffering Olympics," and nobody wins a gold medal.

The truth is, human suffering doesn't work on a comparison scale. Your pain doesn't become invalid just because someone else's might be more intense or widespread. Your nervous system doesn't care that children are starving elsewhere when you lose your job. Your grief doesn't diminish because others have "more legitimate" reasons to mourn.

Yet we persist in this comparative misery, partly because we've been trained to. How many times have you heard phrases like:

"Think of the starving children in [insert impoverished country]!" "At least you have a roof over your head." "It could always be worse." "First world problems."

These dismissals aren't just annoying—they're actively harmful. They create a culture where we invalidate our own emotions and needs, where we feel guilty for normal human reactions, where we minimize legitimate suffering because it doesn't seem "bad enough."

The result? We don't process our emotions. We don't address our needs. We don't heal our wounds. We just stuff them down with a hefty side of shame.

And here's the great irony: this comparative approach to suffering doesn't actually help anyone. It doesn't redirect resources to those who are objectively worse off. It doesn't create more empathy. It just silences conversations that need to happen and prevents people from seeking the support they need.

The Weird Hierarchy of Suffering We've Created

Our society has developed an unspoken ranking system for suffering. Some types of pain are deemed worthy of attention and sympathy, while others are dismissed or even mocked.

Physical illness typically ranks higher than mental illness. Sudden catastrophes get more sympathy than chronic struggles. Certain diagnoses are "acceptable," while others carry stigma. Pain with visible manifestations trumps invisible suffering.

We even rank people's worthiness to suffer. Children's pain matters more than adults'. The suffering of the blameless is valid; the suffering of those who "brought it on themselves" is not. The pain of the privileged is trivial; the pain of the marginalized is expected.

These hierarchies don't just exist between individuals—we internalize them and use them against ourselves. We become our own suffering gatekeepers, deciding whether our pain has earned the right to be acknowledged.

I once had a client who was going through a devastating divorce while her mother was battling cancer. She told me, "I have no right to be upset about my marriage when my mom might die." As if her heart could only hold grief for one loss at a time. As if her own pain was somehow disrespectful to her mother's.

This "suffering hierarchy" shows up everywhere once you start looking for it:

- In workplaces, where some reasons for taking time off are considered valid while others are questioned
- In healthcare, where certain conditions are taken seriously and others are dismissed
- In families, where some members' struggles receive attention while others' are minimized
- In social circles, where certain disclosures are met with support while others create awkward silences

And most perniciously, in our own minds, where we rank our worthiness to receive care based on how our suffering compares to others'.

The Oppression Olympics: When Identity Enters the Chat

This ranking of suffering gets even more complicated when we factor in social identity and systemic oppression. Enter the "Oppression Olympics"—the competitive comparison of different forms of discrimination and marginalization.

The underlying logic goes something like this: The more oppressed your group is, the more legitimate your pain and the more attention your suffering deserves.

This framework isn't completely baseless. Systemic oppression is real. Different groups do face different barriers and harms based on their identities. Intersecting marginalized identities often do create compounded challenges.

But turning this reality into a competition has some serious downsides:

1. It pits marginalized groups against each other instead of focusing on the systems that harm them all

2. It reduces complex human experiences to simplistic identity categories
3. It creates a culture where people feel they need to emphasize their trauma to be taken seriously
4. It discourages solidarity and encourages division

We need to recognize how different forms of oppression operate without falling into the trap of ranking them. We need to acknowledge that privilege in one area doesn't negate suffering in another. We need to validate specific experiences while recognizing our common humanity.

In other words: your suffering matters whether or not you're part of a marginalized group, AND systemic oppression creates additional burdens that need acknowledgment and action.

The Trauma One-Upmanship

Have you ever been in a conversation that turned into a trauma competition? Someone mentions a difficult experience, and suddenly everyone's sharing progressively worse stories, like some macabre game of "top this."

"My boss yelled at me today." "That's nothing. My boss threw a stapler at me once." "Well, my former boss got me blacklisted from the entire industry."

This isn't connection. It's trauma one-upmanship. And it's exhausting.

There's a difference between sharing experiences to validate someone else's feelings ("I've been through something similar and it was hard") and sharing to minimize them ("That's nothing compared to what I went through").

The first creates connection. The second creates distance.

What makes this particularly tricky is that sometimes people engage in trauma one-upmanship without realizing it. They think they're bonding by sharing their own experiences, not recognizing how it comes across as dismissive.

And sometimes, to be perfectly honest, we do it because pain can become a perverse form of social currency—especially in spaces where having overcome adversity is valued. Being the person who "had it worst" can become a strange source of identity and even pride.

But trauma isn't a badge of honor, and suffering isn't a competition. When we treat it that way, we create environments where:

- People feel they need to exaggerate their pain to be taken seriously
- Genuine healing gets sidelined in favor of trauma storytelling
- Hierarchy replaces genuine empathy
- We focus on who has suffered more rather than how we might all suffer less

Finding Your Way Back to Your Own Experience

So how do we escape this comparison trap? How do we validate our own suffering without minimizing others'? How do we acknowledge systemic inequities without creating oppression hierarchies?

The answer begins with a simple recognition: **Pain is pain.**

Your nervous system doesn't calculate your suffering based on how it compares to others'. When you're in pain, you're in pain. Full stop.

This doesn't mean all suffering is identical or that systemic factors don't matter. But it does mean that the subjective experience of suffering deserves compassion regardless of its cause or context.

Think of it this way: If you break your arm, the pain isn't lessened by the fact that someone else broke both legs. If you're grieving a divorce, that grief isn't invalidated by someone else grieving a death. Different wounds, same need for healing.

Here are some practical steps to reconnect with your own experience:

1. Notice the comparison reflex

Pay attention to when you start minimizing your own suffering through comparison. Just noticing this habit is the first step to changing it.

"I notice I'm telling myself I shouldn't feel bad because others have it worse."

2. Validate your own experience

Give yourself permission to acknowledge your pain without qualification.

"This is hard for me right now, and that's a valid feeling regardless of what others are experiencing."

3. Hold complexity

Recognize that you can honor your own suffering AND acknowledge others' pain. It's not either/or.

"I can care about my own struggles AND care about larger issues in the world."

4. Beware of toxic gratitude

There's a difference between genuine gratitude and forced positivity that denies your reality. True gratitude can coexist with pain; toxic gratitude tries to replace it.

"I can be grateful for what I have while still acknowledging what hurts."

5. Check your selective comparisons

Notice that we tend to compare ourselves only to those who seem to have it worse in specific ways, not those who have it better. This selective comparison serves to invalidate our feelings rather than gain perspective.

"If I'm going to compare, I should be fair about it— but better yet, I can choose not to compare at all."

6. Create suffering-competition-free zones

With trusted friends, explicitly agree not to minimize each other's pain through comparison. Give each other permission to feel whatever you feel without ranking it.

"In this friendship, there's no such thing as 'not bad enough' to talk about."

Beyond Comparison: Authentic Compassion

When we move beyond comparing suffering, something remarkable happens: we become capable of more authentic compassion, both for ourselves and others.

True compassion doesn't require ranking pain. It doesn't need to determine who deserves more care. It simply responds to suffering wherever it exists—including our own.

This more expansive approach to compassion recognizes that:

- Different types of suffering require different responses without one being more "legitimate" than another
- Someone's pain being "worse" doesn't make your pain "not real"

- Being privileged in some ways doesn't make your suffering meaningless
- Being oppressed doesn't make suffering your defining characteristic

We can hold awareness of systemic inequities while still honoring individual experiences. We can acknowledge differences in circumstance without creating a hierarchy of who deserves compassion.

The real question isn't "Is my suffering bad enough to count?" but rather "What kind of response does this particular suffering need?"

Sometimes that response is individual: self-care, therapy, rest. Sometimes it's systemic: advocacy, policy change, community support. Most often, it's both.

But it starts with refusing to participate in the Suffering Olympics—with ourselves or others. It starts with recognizing that pain is not a competitive sport, and compassion is not a limited resource.

Your disaster doesn't need to be the worst disaster to deserve care. It just needs to be yours.

CHAPTER 3: The Five Stages of Apocalypse Grief

In 1969, psychiatrist Elisabeth Kübler-Ross introduced the world to her five stages of grief: denial, anger, bargaining, depression, and acceptance. She developed this framework while working with terminally ill patients, but it's since been applied to all kinds of loss—from death and divorce to job loss and major life transitions.

What Kübler-Ross didn't anticipate was that one day, we'd need to apply her framework to a different kind of grief altogether: apocalypse grief. The particular kind of mourning that comes with watching systems collapse, futures evaporate, and certainties dissolve. The grief that accompanies not just personal losses, but collective ones.

Let's be clear: Kübler-Ross herself later emphasized that grief doesn't follow a neat, linear progression. People bounce between stages, skip some entirely, or experience several simultaneously. Grief is messy, not methodical. But the framework still offers a useful map for understanding our emotional responses to overwhelming situations.

So let's explore how the five stages show up when we're grieving not just individual losses, but the larger apocalypses unfolding around us.

Denial: "This Is Fine" (While Sitting in Flames)

You've probably seen that meme—the cartoon dog sitting in a burning room, mug in hand, saying "This is fine" while flames engulf everything. It's funny because it's painfully relatable. We've all been that dog.

Denial is the psychological equivalent of noise-canceling headphones in a hurricane. It's the part of you that keeps scrolling past climate disaster headlines. The part that says "it can't happen here" even as it begins happening everywhere. The part that maintains business-as-usual in decidedly unusual times.

Denial shows up in many forms:

- **Outright rejection:** "The science isn't settled." "It's all media hysteria." "Things have always been this way."

- **Minimization:** "It's not that bad." "This will blow over soon." "We've survived worse."

- **Distraction:** Immersing yourself in work, entertainment, or substances to avoid thinking about what's happening.

- **Compartmentalization:** Acknowledging the problem intellectually while emotionally proceeding as if nothing has changed.

Denial isn't necessarily conscious. Your brain is trying to protect you from information that feels too threatening to process all at once. When reality exceeds our capacity to cope, denial buys us time.

But denial has diminishing returns. The longer we sit in that burning room insisting everything is fine, the fewer options we have for getting out.

I had a friend who ignored the strange sounds her car was making for weeks. "It's probably nothing," she kept saying. By the time she finally acknowledged the problem, what could have been a simple fix had become a complete engine replacement.

The same principle applies to larger crises. Early climate denial has led to more extreme mitigation measures being necessary now. Initial pandemic denial cost countless lives. Financial denial often transforms manageable debts into bankruptcy.

Moving beyond denial doesn't mean constant panic. It means developing a relationship with reality that's neither avoidant nor overwhelming. It means looking at what's happening clearly enough to respond appropriately.

Some questions to help recognize denial:

- What information am I consistently scrolling past or changing the channel on?
- What topics make me immediately change the subject?

- Where in my life am I saying "it'll be fine" without evidence?
- What would it cost me to acknowledge certain realities?
- What uncomfortable emotions might be hiding behind my "it's not that bad" statements?

Denial isn't a character flaw—it's a coping mechanism. But like any coping mechanism, it can outlive its usefulness. When we're ready, we can thank denial for the buffer it provided and move toward a more honest relationship with our situation.

Which often leads us straight into...

Anger: Righteous Rage as Fuel

One morning, I found myself screaming at my phone. Not into it—at it. The device itself had become the target of my rage after yet another notification about environmental regulations being gutted. The headlines had finally penetrated my denial, and anger came rushing in like a flash flood.

Anger is the emotional equivalent of a fire alarm. It alerts us that something is wrong and demands our attention. And in a world where plenty is wrong, anger is not only appropriate—it can be clarifying.

Apocalypse anger takes many forms:

- **Righteous rage:** Fury at those causing or exacerbating crises for profit or power
- **Betrayal:** Anger at institutions that were supposed to protect us but failed
- **Displaced anger:** Snapping at loved ones over minor issues when the real source is bigger
- **Self-directed anger:** Blaming yourself for not doing enough, knowing enough, or acting soon enough
- **Existential anger:** Rage at the universe for putting us in this situation in the first place

Unlike denial, which numbs us to reality, anger fully acknowledges that something is wrong. That's progress! Anger says, "This shouldn't be happening, and I refuse to pretend it's okay."

The problem comes not with feeling anger, but with getting stuck there. Perpetual rage is exhausting. It burns us out. It damages relationships. It can make us reactive rather than responsive.

But anger, channeled effectively, can be powerful fuel for change. The civil rights movement, women's suffrage, environmental protections—all were powered in part by righteous indignation at injustice.

The key is learning to use anger without being consumed by it. To let it inform your actions without dictating them. To transform raw rage into focused resolve.

Some ways to work with anger productively:

- **Name it specifically:** "I'm angry that corporations knew about climate change decades ago and actively worked to suppress the information."

- **Find the underlying values:** Anger often points to what we care about most. "I'm angry because I value truth, accountability, and a livable planet for future generations."

- **Channel it into action:** "I'll use this anger to fuel my involvement with organizations pushing for corporate accountability."

- **Set anger boundaries:** Decide when, where, and how you'll engage with infuriating information. Maybe you don't read the news right before bed, or you limit social media time.

- **Create rage rituals:** Find physical, creative, or social outlets for anger. Exercise, art, protest, community organizing—whatever helps transform anger into something constructive.

Remember: anger isn't the problem. Injustice is the problem. Anger is just the messenger letting you know something needs to change.

As we process our anger, we often move into trying to negotiate our way out of pain...

Bargaining: The Fallacy of "If I Just Recycle Harder..."

"If I just use metal straws and bring my own grocery bags, everything will be okay."

"If I donate to the right organizations, I can offset the damage."

"If I become the perfect climate citizen, I'll have done my part."

Recognize these thoughts? Welcome to the bargaining stage of apocalypse grief.

Bargaining is the "let's make a deal" phase. It's our attempt to regain control over uncontrollable situations by striking imaginary agreements with fate, God, the universe, or ourselves. If I do X, then surely Y won't happen.

In individual grief, bargaining might look like "If I had just made him go to the doctor sooner..." or "If I promise to be a better person, maybe we can work things out." In apocalypse grief, it often manifests as:

- **Individual responsibility hyperfocus:** Believing your personal choices alone can solve systemic problems
- **Perfectionism:** Setting impossible standards for your own environmental/political/social behavior
- **Magical thinking:** Convincing yourself that if you worry enough, prepare enough, or care enough, catastrophe won't touch you

- **Guilt spirals:** Agonizing over every "wrong" choice as if it might tip the scales toward disaster

There's something comforting about bargaining. It creates the illusion that we have more control than we actually do. If disaster happens because I didn't try hard enough, then theoretically, trying harder could prevent it.

This isn't entirely irrational. Individual actions do matter. Your choices do have impacts. But bargaining becomes problematic when it:

1. Places systemic burdens entirely on individual shoulders
2. Creates eco-anxiety and perfectionism that ultimately leads to burnout
3. Distracts from collective action that might actually create meaningful change
4. Becomes a form of performative virtue rather than effective action

I had a client who developed debilitating anxiety about her carbon footprint. She stopped traveling to see family, refused to buy new clothes even when needed, and berated herself for every slip-up. Her bargaining had become a prison. Meanwhile, she had no energy left for community organizing or systemic advocacy—the very things that might have made a bigger difference.

Some signs you might be stuck in bargaining:

- You feel personally responsible for fixing massive global problems
- You judge yourself harshly for imperfect environmental/political choices
- You believe if you just find the perfect combination of individual actions, you can ensure safety
- You spend more time on symbolic actions than effective ones
- You feel guilty taking any time to enjoy life while crises exist

Moving beyond bargaining doesn't mean abandoning personal responsibility. It means right-sizing it. It means understanding that while individual choices matter, collective action and systemic change matter more. It means replacing "If I just..." with "While I do what I can, I also recognize the need for larger solutions."

When bargaining fails to deliver the control and safety we crave, we often slide into...

Depression: When the Weight of the World Crushes Your Sofa

There was a week in 2021 when I didn't get off my couch except for absolute necessities. The pandemic was raging, climate disasters were multiplying, democracy seemed to be crumbling, and I hit a wall. The weight of it all physically pressed me into my cushions. I stared at the ceiling and thought, "What's the point?"

That's depression—the "this is too much" stage of grief. It's the emotional equivalent of your computer displaying the blue screen of death. System overload. Shutdown initiated.

Apocalypse depression isn't the same as clinical depression (though they can certainly overlap and reinforce each other). It's a natural response to overwhelming loss and threat. When the gap between the world we expected and the world we're getting becomes too vast, depression often fills the space.

This stage of grief shows up as:

- **Emotional numbness:** Feeling disconnected from things that once brought joy
- **Fatalism:** "We're doomed anyway, so why bother?"
- **Withdrawal:** Retreating from news, social connections, and engagement
- **Exhaustion:** Profound physical and emotional tiredness that sleep doesn't seem to fix
- **Loss of meaning:** Questioning the point of work, relationships, or efforts that once seemed important

Depression in this context is often a response to legitimate losses—loss of certainty, loss of future plans, loss of faith in institutions, loss of environmental stability, loss of a world we thought we understood.

It's important to distinguish depression as a grief stage from clinical depression requiring professional treatment. While they share symptoms, grief depression typically shifts over time, especially with processing and support. If your depression persists, intensifies, or includes thoughts of harming yourself, please seek professional help immediately. (Resources are listed in the appendix.)

That said, even situational depression requires care and attention. Some approaches that can help:

- **Honor the losses:** Name specifically what you're grieving. "I'm grieving the future I thought my children would have." "I'm grieving my faith in certain institutions." "I'm grieving the natural world as I knew it."

- **Connect with others:** Depression isolates, but connection heals. Find people who can sit with your difficult feelings without trying to immediately fix or dismiss them.

- **Gentle movement:** Even five minutes of walking, stretching, or dancing can shift brain chemistry and provide temporary relief.

- **Create tiny pockets of meaning:** Depression makes everything seem pointless. Counter this by creating small, manageable moments of purpose or joy— helping one person, tending one plant, creating one small beautiful thing.

- **Lower the bar temporarily:** During acute depression, "good enough" is perfect. Basic self-care, rest, and reaching out when possible are victories.

Remember: depression in response to legitimate global crises isn't a mental health failure. It's your psyche processing enormous challenges. Treat yourself with the compassion you'd offer anyone navigating profound loss.

As we move through depression, we eventually reach...

Acceptance: Not Giving Up, But Giving In to Reality

There's a common misconception that acceptance means resignation—that we're throwing up our hands and saying, "Oh well, apocalypse it is!"

That's not what acceptance means in grief work. Acceptance isn't giving up—it's giving in to reality. It's acknowledging what is so we can respond appropriately rather than waste energy fighting the fact that it's happening at all.

Acceptance in apocalypse grief looks like:

- **Clear-eyed assessment:** Seeing threats for what they are—not minimized, not catastrophized
- **Present-moment orientation:** Dealing with what's actually happening now rather than constantly projecting worst-case scenarios
- **Flexible planning:** Making adaptive plans that can change as circumstances do
- **Both/and thinking:** Holding that things can be both terrible and beautiful, hopeless and hopeful, ending and beginning simultaneously
- **Right-sized responsibility:** Taking appropriate action without shouldering the burden of fixing everything

Acceptance doesn't mean you like what's happening. It doesn't mean you approve of it or think it's okay. It simply means you're no longer spending energy denying, raging against, bargaining with, or collapsing under the weight of it. You're standing firmly in what is and responding from there.

I remember the moment I reached a form of climate acceptance. After cycling through denial

("The scientists must be exaggerating"), anger ("How dare corporations do this to our planet!"), bargaining ("If I live a zero-waste lifestyle, it will make a difference"), and depression ("We're doomed anyway"), I landed somewhere different.

I acknowledged that yes, significant climate damage is locked in. And no, my individual actions alone won't fix it. And yes, powerful interests continue to block necessary change. AND YET... there are still meaningful actions worth taking. There are still futures worth fighting for. There is still joy to be found in the midst of it all.

Acceptance created space for complexity. Instead of oscillating between naive optimism and total despair, I could hold a more nuanced position: This is really bad AND we don't know exactly how the story ends AND what we do still matters.

Some pathways to acceptance:

- **Practice cognitive flexibility:** Notice when you're thinking in all-or-nothing terms about crises. Look for the gray areas, the contradictions, the unexpected possibilities.

- **Cultivate present-moment awareness:** When you find yourself catastrophizing about the future or ruminating about past mistakes, gently bring yourself back to what's actually happening right now, in this moment.

- **Embrace uncertainty:** Practice sitting with not knowing exactly how things will unfold. Uncertainty is uncomfortable but opens us to possibilities that rigid predictions don't.

- **Find role models:** Look for people who acknowledge harsh realities while continuing to live with purpose and even joy. They demonstrate that acceptance doesn't mean surrendering to despair.

- **Right-size your sphere of influence:** Focus primarily on what you can affect while staying informed about the bigger picture. Not ignoring larger systems, but not being paralyzed by them either.

Acceptance isn't a destination you reach once and for all. It's a practice, a relationship with reality that requires constant renewal as circumstances change. You'll likely revisit other grief stages as new information emerges or new losses occur. That's normal.

The point isn't to achieve perfect acceptance and never experience denial, anger, bargaining, or depression again. The point is to move through these stages with increasing skill rather than getting permanently stuck in any one of them.

Beyond the Five Stages: Integration

While Kübler-Ross's model ends with acceptance, many grief therapists now recognize another important phase: integration. This is where loss becomes part of your story rather than the whole story.

Integration in apocalypse grief might look like:

- Developing new skills and communities in response to changing conditions
- Finding purpose in creating better systems rather than merely preserving old ones
- Holding space for both grief and joy, concern and hope, endings and beginnings
- Creating meaningful rituals and practices that acknowledge both loss and continuity

- Building identity and meaning that incorporate rather than deny difficult realities

Integration doesn't erase grief; it transforms it into something that can coexist with a purposeful life. The apocalypse becomes part of your story—an important part, but not the only part.

As teacher and activist adrienne maree brown writes, "Things are not getting worse, they are getting uncovered. We must hold each other tight and continue to pull back the veil."

Integration means neither covering the hard truths back up nor being overwhelmed by their exposure. It means seeing clearly and still finding ways to create, connect, and care.

In the chapters ahead, we'll explore practical ways to cultivate cozy spaces of meaning, joy, and purpose amid the apocalypse—not despite our grief, but alongside it. Because acceptance doesn't mean resignation. It means dealing with what is while still working toward what could be.

And sometimes, even in apocalypse, what could be is beautiful.

CHAPTER 4: Creating Pockets of Peace

In the midst of chaos, we all need sanctuaries. Not permanent escapes—those don't exist—but temporary shelters where we can catch our breath, restore our energy, and remember what we're fighting for in the first place.

I call these "pockets of peace"—small, intentional spaces of calm in an otherwise turbulent world. They're not about ignoring reality or pretending everything is fine. They're about creating sustainable conditions for continued engagement with difficult circumstances.

Think of it like this: Even in actual war zones, soldiers don't fight 24/7. They have rest periods, base camps, moments of downtime. If people in literal combat need breaks, why would we expect ourselves to face metaphorical apocalypses without respite?

In this chapter, we'll explore how to create these essential pockets of peace in three domains: your physical space, your digital life, and your internal landscape. None of these require significant resources or special skills—just intention and permission to prioritize your wellbeing.

Designing Your Physical Space for Maximum Calm in Chaos

Our physical environments affect us more profoundly than we realize. Research consistently shows that our surroundings impact everything from our stress levels and cognitive function to our mood and sleep quality. While we can't control the larger environments we move through, most of us can make at least small adjustments to our immediate surroundings.

Let's start with where you live. Whether you have an entire house or just a corner of a shared room, consider:

1. Create a "low-stimulus zone"

Our brains are constantly processing sensory information, and in our hyper-connected world, we're typically overstimulated. Counteract this by designating at least one area (even if it's just a chair) as a low-stimulus zone.

This might mean:

- Minimal visual clutter
- Softer lighting (especially avoiding blue light)
- Reduced noise (or specific calming sounds)
- Comfortable textures
- Pleasant but subtle scents

I have a friend who transformed a closet into a "panic pod" with pillows, fairy lights, and noise-canceling headphones. Another created a reading nook by simply hanging a curtain around a corner of her bedroom. My own low-stimulus zone is just my bedroom with a strict "no phones, no news" rule after 9 PM.

The goal isn't Instagram-worthy perfection or expensive renovations. It's creating a space where your nervous system can downregulate—where the constant alerts of potential threat can temporarily quiet.

2. Incorporate natural elements

Numerous studies confirm what many of us intuitively know: nature calms us. While not everyone has access to outdoor spaces, most of us can bring small elements of nature into our homes:

- Houseplants (even hard-to-kill varieties like snake plants or pothos)
- Natural materials (wood, stone, clay, wool)
- Natural light when possible
- Images of nature (even photographs of landscapes can provide some benefit)
- Sounds of nature (rainfall, ocean waves, forest sounds)

During particularly stressful periods, I keep a small collection of stones on my desk. Touching their cool, smooth surfaces while taking a few deep breaths provides a surprising amount of grounding.

3. Create comfort clusters

Strategically place "comfort clusters" around your living space—small groupings of items that provide sensory comfort or meaningful connection. These might include:

- A soft blanket and supportive cushion
- A favorite mug and special tea

- A scented candle and matches
- A small album of happy photos
- A journal and good pen
- A meaningful object that connects you to someone you love

The key is having these comfort stations readily available without effort. When we're already overwhelmed, having to search for comforting items requires energy we may not have. Make comfort the path of least resistance.

4. Consider the transition zones

The spaces between environments—the threshold of your home, the area where you remove your work clothes, the place you set down your keys— deserve special attention. These transition zones can help you consciously shift between different modes of being.

Some ideas:

- Place something beautiful or calming by your entrance door
- Create a small "decompression ritual" for returning home (removing shoes, washing hands, changing clothes)
- Designate a specific place for items that carry stress (work bags, phones, mail)

- Mark the boundary between work and personal space, even if it's just a different chair

A therapist I know keeps a small bowl of water by her front door. Each time she enters, she dips her fingers in and symbolically "washes off" whatever energy she's bringing from outside. It's a simple ritual that creates psychological space between worlds.

5. Embrace imperfection and limitations

If you're reading about creating calm spaces while surrounded by toys, roommates, piles of laundry, or other realities that seem incompatible with tranquility, please know this: Perfection is not the point. Intention is.

Maybe your pocket of peace is just your headphones and a playlist that helps you feel calm. Maybe it's the five minutes you spend in your car before entering your chaotic home. Maybe it's a corner of your kitchen table cleared just long enough to enjoy a cup of tea.

Work with what you have. Start where you are. Even tiny adjustments can make a difference in how you experience your environment.

As one of my clients who lives in a small apartment with three children puts it: "My pocket of peace is the bathroom with the door locked and a five-minute meditation app. It's not Instagram-worthy, but it keeps me sane."

Digital Bunkers: Protecting Your Mind from the Information Hellscape

While our physical environments certainly affect us, many of us spend just as much (if not more) time in digital environments. Our devices connect us to infinite information, much of it specifically designed to trigger strong emotional responses. Creating digital pockets of peace is just as important as creating physical ones.

1. Audit your information diet

Just as you would examine what foods you're putting into your body, take an honest look at what information you're consuming:

- What sources do you regularly check?
- How do you feel during and after consuming different types of content?

- What percentage of your media consumption leaves you feeling informed versus merely agitated?
- What's the balance between news about problems and information about solutions?
- How much information is actionable versus simply alarming?

This isn't about ignoring important issues. It's about being intentional regarding how, when, and in what proportion you consume different types of information.

2. Create boundaries around consumption

Once you've assessed your information diet, establish some boundaries:

- Designate specific times for news consumption rather than constant checking
- Consider a "no screens" policy for certain spaces (bedroom, dining table) or times (first hour after waking, last hour before sleep)
- Use technology to limit technology (screen time settings, website blockers, app timers)
- Create a "information consumption ritual" that helps you prepare for and process difficult content

I have a client who allows herself 30 minutes of news in the morning, but only after meditation and breakfast. Another reads news only on weekdays, giving himself weekends to process and rest. I check news twice daily at scheduled times, never first thing in the morning or right before bed.

3. Curate digital sanctuaries

Within your digital life, intentionally create spaces of rest, beauty, or meaningful connection:

- Playlists that calm or uplift you
- Folders of photos that bring you joy
- Podcasts that leave you feeling centered or inspired
- Digital communities focused on solutions, beauty, or support
- Apps designed for meditation, nature sounds, or creative expression

Think of these as digital oases you can visit when you need a break from the information desert.

4. Practice digital minimalism

Consider simplifying your digital environment:

- Unfollow accounts that consistently leave you feeling worse
- Unsubscribe from emails that don't serve you

- Organize apps so the most calming ones are easily accessible
- Remove notifications for all but the most essential functions
- Regularly clear digital clutter (old files, screenshots, downloads)

Just as physical clutter can overwhelm our senses, digital clutter can overwhelm our attention and emotional capacity.

5. Create transition rituals

Develop small rituals that help you transition between digital and physical reality:

- Take three deep breaths before checking your phone in the morning
- Stretch or shake out your body after long periods online
- Look at something 20 feet away for 20 seconds every 20 minutes (the 20-20-20 rule for eye strain)
- Have a specific phrase or action that marks the end of your digital consumption time

These transitions help your nervous system register shifts between different modes of attention and presence.

6. Remember your power

Perhaps most importantly, remind yourself regularly that you have agency in your digital life. You are not powerless against algorithms and attention engineers. You get to decide what enters your awareness, when, and how much space it occupies.

This isn't about perfect digital hygiene—we all get sucked into doomscrolling sometimes. It's about remembering that your attention is precious and limited. You have both the right and the responsibility to steward it carefully.

The Power of Ridiculously Small Comforts

Before we move on to internal peace practices, let's talk about something that might seem trivial but is actually essential: small comforts.

In disaster response work, there's a concept called "psychological first aid." It recognizes that during crises, basic comforts aren't luxuries—they're necessities for psychological functioning. Warm drinks, blankets, familiar objects—these things help stabilize people during acute stress.

What we're experiencing now is often a form of chronic, low-grade disaster. The psychological principles still apply.

This is why seemingly small comforts—a particular tea, a soft blanket, a familiar scent, a favorite song —can have outsized impacts on our wellbeing. They're not indulgences; they're legitimate coping tools.

Some examples of small comforts that can create momentary pockets of peace:

- Warm beverages (the ritual of preparation as much as the drink itself)
- Specific textures against your skin (soft blankets, smooth stones, warm water)
- Gentle pressure (weighted blankets, firm hugs, layered clothing)
- Particular scents (candles, essential oils, fresh air, baked goods)
- Familiar sounds (rainfall, certain music, purring cats, crackling fires)
- Taste experiences (a square of chocolate, a slice of fruit, a spoonful of peanut butter)
- Visual anchors (a photograph, a plant, a view, a particular color)

The most effective small comforts often engage multiple senses simultaneously, giving our overactive minds several different inputs to process instead of spinning on worries.

What makes these "ridiculously small" comforts so powerful is their accessibility. You don't need special circumstances, significant time, or extra resources to experience them. They can be integrated into ordinary life, creating micro-moments of peace throughout your day.

I want to emphasize this point because I've seen too many wellbeing resources that assume everyone has time for hour-long baths or money for massage therapy or physical ability for yoga. While those are wonderful if accessible to you, peace shouldn't be a privilege only available to those with certain resources.

Ridiculously small comforts are democratic. Almost everyone can access at least some form of sensory comfort that grounds them in their body and momentarily eases their mental burden.

Make a list of your own small comforts. Keep it on your phone or somewhere easily accessible. When you feel overwhelmed, choose one thing from your list—just one tiny, doable action that might create a moment of peace.

Remember: We're not aiming for hours of bliss here. We're creating tiny pockets of peace that, over time, help maintain our capacity to face difficult realities.

Building Internal Sanctuaries

While physical and digital environments significantly impact our wellbeing, ultimately, we carry our experience within us. Learning to create internal pockets of peace—mental and emotional spaces of calm—may be the most portable and resilient strategy of all.

1. Mindful awareness practices

At its core, mindfulness is simply the practice of paying attention to your present experience without judgment. Despite becoming somewhat of a buzzword, the research supporting its benefits for stress reduction is substantial.

You don't need to meditate for hours or master complex techniques. Even brief moments of mindful awareness can create small pockets of internal peace:

- Pause to notice your breathing for three conscious breaths

- Feel the sensation of your feet connecting with the ground as you walk
- Notice the temperature, texture, and taste of your food as you eat
- Observe the physical sensations of emotions in your body
- Listen to the layers of sound in your environment

The key is bringing full attention to your immediate experience rather than being caught in thoughts about the past or future. This doesn't make problems disappear, but it can create a bit of space around them.

2. Mental refuge visualization

Our brains don't always distinguish clearly between what we imagine and what we experience. This means visualization can create genuine physiological effects similar to actually being in a peaceful environment.

Create a detailed mental image of a place—real or imagined—where you feel completely safe and at peace. It might be a childhood home, a favorite natural setting, or an entirely fictional sanctuary. Develop this image with as much sensory detail as possible:

- What do you see? (Colors, light, shapes, movement)
- What do you hear? (Natural sounds, music, silence)
- What do you feel? (Textures, temperature, air movement)
- What do you smell? (Plants, food, clean air)
- What do you taste? (If relevant)

Practice visiting this mental refuge regularly so it becomes easier to access during stressful moments. The more you rehearse this visualization, the more effective it becomes as a quick reset for your nervous system.

3. Narrative reframing

The stories we tell ourselves about what's happening significantly impact our experience. While toxic positivity demands we ignore reality in favor of forced optimism, healthy reframing acknowledges reality while finding constructive perspectives within it.

Some reframing approaches that can create internal pockets of peace:

- Looking for meaning amid difficulty ("This is hard AND it's teaching me important things")

- Identifying what remains within your control when much feels uncontrollable
- Recognizing temporality ("This intense feeling will pass, even if the situation remains")
- Connecting personal experiences to larger human experiences ("Others have faced similar challenges")
- Finding the "both/and" instead of "either/or" ("This is painful AND there are still moments of beauty")

The goal isn't to deny reality but to hold it in a way that allows for agency and meaning.

4. Body-based regulation

Our bodies and minds are inseparably connected. Sometimes the quickest route to mental calm is through physical regulation:

- Deep, slow breathing (especially extending the exhale)
- Progressive muscle relaxation (tensing and releasing muscle groups)
- Rhythmic movement (walking, swaying, rocking, dancing)
- Temperature changes (cool water on the face, warm hands, etc.)
- Bilateral stimulation (tapping alternating sides of the body)

These aren't just psychological tricks—they directly affect your nervous system, helping shift from fight-flight-freeze responses toward more regulated states.

5. Micro-meaning practices

Finding moments of meaning amid chaos provides significant psychological protection. Research on resilience consistently shows that purpose and meaning correlate with ability to withstand adversity.

Create small, daily practices that connect you to what matters most:

- Brief gratitude identification (specific and authentic, not forced)
- Small acts of creation (making something, anything)
- Moments of genuine connection (even brief or virtual)
- Tiny contributions to causes you care about
- Brief reflection on personal values and how they manifest even in difficult times

These don't need to be grand gestures. A text checking on a friend, planting a single seed, writing one paragraph of reflection—small actions add up to a meaningful life, even in apocalyptic times.

Bringing It All Together: Your Personal Peace Plan

Now that we've explored physical, digital, and internal approaches to creating pockets of peace, let's put them together into a personalized plan. Remember, this isn't about achieving perfect tranquility in a chaotic world—it's about creating just enough calm to allow you to engage sustainably with difficult realities.

Step 1: Identify your personal peace disruptors

What specifically tends to activate your stress response? Common examples include:

- Certain types of news or social media
- Particular physical environments
- Specific interpersonal dynamics
- Time pressure or scheduling issues
- Bodily states (hunger, fatigue, pain)
- Financial concerns
- Specific topics or triggers related to past experiences

The more precisely you can identify what disrupts your peace, the more effectively you can create targeted pockets of calm.

Step 2: Notice your peace indicators

How do you know when you're experiencing a moment of peace? What sensations, thoughts, or feelings indicate that your nervous system is in a more regulated state?

Common peace indicators include:

- Deeper breathing
- Relaxed muscles
- Ability to focus
- Emotional stability
- Sense of perspective
- Physical comfort
- Mental clarity

Identifying these indicators helps you recognize what actually works for you, rather than what's supposed to work according to generic advice.

Step 3: Create your peace portfolio

Develop a diverse collection of peace practices that address different needs, contexts, and levels of accessibility:

- **Emergency peace practices:** Ultra-simple techniques you can use anywhere, anytime, even in the midst of acute stress (example: five deep breaths while counting)

- **Daily peace anchors:** Small, consistent practices you can integrate into your existing routine to create regular moments of calm (example: a three-minute morning ritual of stretching and setting intentions)

- **Deep peace resources:** More immersive practices for when you have more time and capacity (example: a weekend afternoon spent in nature without devices)

Having options at different levels ensures you can access some form of peace practice regardless of circumstances.

Step 4: Implement preventive peace

Rather than waiting until you're already overwhelmed, proactively create pockets of peace throughout your day:

- Schedule brief calm breaks between activities
- Set peace anchors in your physical space to remind you to pause

- Create transition rituals between different modes (work/home, online/offline)
- Identify predictable stress points and plan peace practices before them

Think of this as regular maintenance for your psychological wellbeing, not just emergency repair.

Step 5: Practice self-compassion when peace feels impossible

There will be times when no peace practice seems to help—when the internal or external chaos is simply too intense. In these moments, self-compassion becomes essential.

Remember:

- Struggling to find peace during genuinely terrible circumstances is normal, not a failure
- Peace is a practice, not a permanent state
- Sometimes the most self-compassionate choice is to acknowledge that this moment is simply hard
- Even when peace feels inaccessible, you can still offer yourself kindness

The Radical Nature of Creating Peace

In a world that profits from your anxiety, that demands constant vigilance, that measures worth by productivity, creating pockets of peace is not merely a self-care strategy—it's a radical act.

When systems rely on your fear, your exhaustion, and your disconnection from yourself, finding moments of calm clarity is subversive. It's reclaiming your autonomy. It's declaring that while you cannot control what happens in the world, you can influence how you experience and respond to it.

This isn't about escaping reality or abdicating responsibility. It's about sustaining yourself for the long journey of living meaningfully in difficult times.

The apocalypse may continue—in fact, it almost certainly will—but within it, you can create pockets of peace. Not despite the chaos, but because of it. Not as denial, but as resistance. Not as surrender, but as sustainability.

In the next chapter, we'll explore how to extend these pockets of peace beyond yourself to create connections with others who can help you navigate these challenging times.

CHAPTER 5: Your Apocalypse Crew

In every disaster movie, there's that pivotal scene where a ragtag group of unlikely allies bands together. The cynical scientist. The practical mechanic. The unexpectedly resilient office worker. The person who's been preparing for this exact scenario for years. Each brings different skills, perspectives, and energies to the collective effort of surviving whatever asteroid/alien/zombie/climate disaster is unfolding.

It's a cinematic trope, sure. But it's also a profound truth about human resilience: we survive better together. In fact, connection isn't just nice to have during difficult times—it's essential.

As researcher and physician Vivek Murthy notes in his book "Together," loneliness is as damaging to physical health as smoking 15 cigarettes a day. During periods of heightened stress and uncertainty, social connection becomes even more vital. It's not just emotional comfort—it's a biological necessity.

The problem? Many of our traditional community structures have eroded. Extended families often live far apart. Religious communities have declined. Neighborhoods are less connected. Work is increasingly remote or transient. The very real apocalypses we're facing are unfolding during what was already an epidemic of loneliness.

This means we need to be intentional about creating our apocalypse crews—the people who will help us navigate these difficult times. Not just any people, but the right people, in the right configurations, with the right expectations.

Let's explore how to find, cultivate, and maintain these essential connections.

Why Chosen Family Matters More Than Ever

The concept of "chosen family" has roots in LGBTQ+ communities, where many individuals, rejected by biological relatives, created alternative family structures based on mutual care and understanding rather than DNA. This concept has profound relevance for all of us navigating apocalyptic times.

When systems fail—whether governmental, economic, or environmental—relationship networks become our most reliable safety nets. Your apocalypse crew might include biological family, but it will likely extend beyond those boundaries to include people connected by shared values, complementary skills, geographic proximity, and mutual commitment.

What makes chosen family different from casual friendship or professional networking is the explicit acknowledgment of interdependence. These are the people you can call at 3 AM. The ones who will check on you during disasters. The ones who see your struggle and show up without being asked. And in turn, these are the people for whom you do the same.

Some benefits of chosen family in apocalyptic times:

1. Resource sharing and practical support

Pooling resources—whether material goods, skills, information, or connections—creates resilience that isolated individuals cannot achieve. During actual disasters like hurricanes or blackouts, neighbors sharing generators, food, or shelter often make the difference between dangerous situations and merely inconvenient ones.

On a more everyday level, chosen family might share childcare, transportation, meals, tools, or knowledge—creating small economies of mutual aid that reduce individual vulnerability to system failures.

2. Emotional co-regulation

Our nervous systems are designed to respond to other nervous systems. When we're in fight-flight-freeze mode, the calm, regulated presence of another person can help bring us back to baseline. This isn't just psychological comfort—it's biological regulation.

Having people who can hold space for your difficult emotions without trying to fix, dismiss, or amplify them is invaluable during apocalyptic times. Equally important is having people who can help you find moments of levity, joy, and meaning amid the chaos.

3. Perspective balancing

None of us sees reality completely clearly, especially under stress. We tend toward our own cognitive biases and emotional patterns. Other people can help us reality-check our thinking, identify blind spots, and consider alternative interpretations.

A well-chosen apocalypse crew will include people with different cognitive styles: the pragmatist who focuses on immediate solutions, the visionary who sees possibilities others miss, the critical thinker who spots potential problems, the emotional intelligence specialist who tracks the human impact of decisions.

4. Identity anchoring

When external circumstances change rapidly, our sense of self can become destabilized. Who are we if our work disappears? If our home is destroyed? If our routine activities become impossible? Chosen family helps anchor our identity through recognition and reflection.

The people who knew you before, who see you clearly now, and who help you imagine who you might become—these connections provide continuity of identity even as external circumstances shift dramatically.

5. Collaborative meaning-making

Humans are meaning-making creatures. We need to make sense of what's happening, especially during chaotic times. Chosen family provides a collaborative space for processing experiences, constructing narratives, and finding purpose amid disruption.

The stories we tell about what's happening and why it matters significantly impact our ability to maintain hope and agency. Having trusted others with whom to develop these narratives is far more effective than trying to create meaning in isolation.

How to Find Your People When Communities Are Fractured

Understanding the importance of chosen family is one thing. Actually finding your people in an increasingly fragmented world is another challenge entirely. Here are some approaches that can help:

1. Start with values alignment rather than demographic similarity

While it's natural to connect with people who share our age, background, or lifestyle, values alignment is a stronger foundation for apocalypse crew relationships. Identify your core values—what matters most to you, especially during difficult times—and look for others who share those priorities.

This doesn't mean finding ideological clones. In fact, some healthy disagreement and diversity of perspective strengthens a group. But fundamental alignment on basic values like mutual aid, respect, compassion, or whatever else you deem essential provides the necessary foundation.

2. Seek out "crisis-revealed" connections

Pay attention to who shows up during smaller crises or challenges. Who checks in when you're sick? Who offers practical help during stressful times? Who can you talk to honestly about difficult emotions? Who makes you feel more capable rather than more overwhelmed?

These "crisis-revealed" connections often provide better information about potential apocalypse crew members than who's fun at parties or shares your taste in movies.

3. Look for complementary coping styles

Different people handle stress in different ways. Some get very practical and action-oriented. Others process emotionally first. Some need community. Others need solitude to recharge.

Rather than seeking people who handle stress exactly like you do, look for those whose coping styles complement yours. If you tend to get lost in catastrophic thinking, friends who excel at practical next steps can be balancing. If you go immediately to solution mode, friends who create space for emotional processing can add an important dimension.

4. Explore mutual aid networks

Formal and informal mutual aid networks—groups explicitly organized around sharing resources and support—can be excellent places to find apocalypse crew members. These might include:

- Neighborhood pods or block associations
- Buy Nothing groups
- Food sharing networks
- Tool libraries
- Skill-sharing communities
- Disaster preparedness groups
- Care collectives for parents, elders, or those with chronic illness

What makes these groups particularly valuable is that they're already organized around the principle of interdependence rather than just social connection.

5. Deepen existing connections

Sometimes we already know people who could be part of our apocalypse crew, but our relationships remain at a relatively surface level. Actively deepening these connections might involve:

- Explicitly discussing mutual support
- Being more vulnerable about real challenges
- Offering specific help rather than vague availability
- Creating regular rhythms of connection

- Working on projects together to test compatibility

Not every friend will become apocalypse crew material, and that's okay. Different relationships serve different purposes. But some existing connections may have untapped potential for deeper mutual support.

6. Create gathering spaces

If you're not finding existing communities that meet your needs, consider creating one. This doesn't have to be elaborate—it could be as simple as a monthly potluck, a weekly walk, or an online space for discussing specific shared interests.

What matters is creating regular, accessible opportunities for connection that have enough structure to reduce social awkwardness but enough flexibility to allow authentic relationships to develop organically.

Setting Boundaries with Doomsday Enthusiasts and Toxic Optimists Alike

Just as important as finding the right people for your apocalypse crew is establishing boundaries with those who deplete rather than restore your capacity to cope. Two particularly challenging types during apocalyptic times are doomsday enthusiasts and toxic optimists.

Doomsday Enthusiasts

We all know them—people who seem almost excited about how terrible everything is, who share every worst-case scenario, who turn every conversation into a recitation of collapse indicators. They're not wrong that things are bad, but their approach can be profoundly depleting.

Signs of doomsday enthusiasm include:

- Sharing alarming information without context or coping strategies
- Dismissing any positive developments as insignificant
- Treating apocalyptic outcomes as foregone conclusions
- Seeming energized rather than appropriately concerned about disasters
- Making predictions with inappropriate certainty
- Criticizing others for not being sufficiently alarmed

Setting boundaries with doomsday enthusiasts might look like:

- Limiting exposure to their content (muting, unfollowing, or reducing in-person time)
- Redirecting conversations toward constructive responses
- Explicitly stating your information limits ("I'm at capacity for disaster news today")
- Finding focused ways to engage that don't involve endless doom-scrolling together
- Requesting balanced perspectives that include both challenges and possibilities

Toxic Optimists

On the other end of the spectrum are toxic optimists—those who insist everything will be fine, who dismiss legitimate concerns, who respond to distress with platitudes rather than understanding. Their relentless positivity can feel invalidating and isolating.

Signs of toxic optimism include:

- Dismissing concerns with phrases like "it'll all work out" without engagement
- Suggesting personal attitude is the primary factor in systemic problems

- Making others feel guilty for expressing worry or grief
- Conflating optimism with moral goodness
- Offering spiritual bypasses for practical problems
- Failing to distinguish between hope (which acknowledges reality) and denial (which doesn't)

Setting boundaries with toxic optimists might look like:

- Clearly stating your need for validation before solutions
- Finding specific people for specific needs (some friends for emotional validation, others for practical optimism)
- Directly requesting space for difficult emotions without immediate reframing
- Distinguishing between hope and denial in your communications
- Being selective about what struggles you share with whom

The Middle Path: Grounded Hope

What we're seeking for our apocalypse crew are neither doomsday enthusiasts nor toxic optimists, but people capable of grounded hope— acknowledging reality while maintaining possibility.

People with grounded hope:

- Face difficult truths without becoming defined by them
- Hold space for grief without getting lost in it
- Take action without requiring certainty about outcomes
- Maintain humor without dismissing seriousness
- Find meaning amid challenge
- Stay engaged without burning out

These are the people who can tell you, "Yes, this is really hard AND we'll figure it out together," and make you believe both parts of that sentence equally.

The Four Types of Relationships Every Apocalypse Crew Needs

While your specific apocalypse crew will be unique to your situation, research on resilient communities suggests that most people benefit from having four distinct types of supportive relationships:

1. The Anchor

This is the person (or people) with whom you have the deepest mutual commitment—the one who knows your fears, hopes, and needs without extensive explanation. The one who has seen you at your worst and remained steadfast.

Anchors provide secure attachment—the psychological home base that allows you to face challenges knowing someone has your back completely. This might be a partner, best friend, sibling, or parent—the defining feature is depth of commitment and understanding rather than specific role.

Having at least one anchor relationship significantly increases resilience during crises. If you don't currently have this type of relationship, it becomes a priority to cultivate, though it typically develops over time rather than immediately.

2. The Practical Supporters

These are the people in your life who excel at tangible help—who will bring soup when you're sick, help you move furniture, feed your pets during an evacuation, or talk through logistical challenges.

Practical supporters may not be your emotional confidants, but their concrete assistance creates essential safety nets. They're often action-oriented people who show care through doing rather than discussing.

Ideally, your apocalypse crew includes several practical supporters with diverse skills and resources, creating redundancy in your support system.

3. The Meaning-Makers

These connections help you process experiences, find perspective, and construct meaningful narratives about what's happening. They're the people who engage with the "why" questions and existential dimensions of apocalyptic times.

Meaning-makers might be spiritually oriented friends, philosophically inclined colleagues, creative companions, or anyone with whom you can explore the deeper implications of current events beyond immediate practical concerns.

These relationships help prevent despair by connecting personal experiences to larger contexts and values.

4. The Joy-Bringers

Perhaps most easily overlooked during apocalyptic times are those relationships centered on pleasure, play, and joy—the people who make you laugh, who share your hobbies, who remember the importance of delight even amid difficulty.

Joy-bringers aren't trivial additions to your apocalypse crew—they're essential for sustainable resilience. They help prevent burnout, maintain perspective, and preserve the very qualities of life worth fighting for.

Your apocalypse crew ideally includes people who fulfill multiple roles, but it's rare for any single person to excel in all four areas. Recognizing the different types of support you need allows you to cultivate a balanced relationship network rather than placing impossible expectations on any one connection.

The Practical Logistics of Crew Maintenance

Building an apocalypse crew isn't a one-time task but an ongoing practice. Here are some practical approaches to maintaining these essential connections:

1. Create regular rhythms of connection

Consistency often matters more than intensity for relationship maintenance. Small, regular connections—a weekly check-in text, a monthly meal, a quarterly deeper conversation—build more resilience than occasional grand gestures.

Consider creating:

- Daily micro-connections with closest ties (brief texts, voice messages)
- Weekly lightweight gatherings (walks, coffee dates, online game sessions)
- Monthly deeper exchanges (shared meals, meaningful conversations)
- Quarterly or annual traditions that mark time together

These rhythms create relationship infrastructure that can withstand the disruptions of apocalyptic times.

2. Be explicit about mutual support

Many of us grew up with implicit relationship models where needs and expectations remained unspoken. This approach breaks down during crises when clarity becomes essential.

Consider having explicit conversations about:

- What forms of support each person needs and can offer
- How to communicate when overwhelmed

- What constitutes an emergency warranting immediate response
- How resources might be shared during difficult times
- What personal boundaries must be respected

These conversations may feel awkward initially but create much more sustainable relationships, preventing misunderstandings and resentment during high-stress periods.

3. Practice reciprocity without scorekeeping

Healthy apocalypse crews operate on the principle of "from each according to their ability, to each according to their need"—recognizing that both ability and need fluctuate over time.

This means:

- Sometimes you'll give more than you receive
- Sometimes you'll receive more than you can give
- The goal is long-term balance, not transaction-by-transaction equality
- Different people contribute different types of support based on their capacities

Practicing this flexible reciprocity requires letting go of rigid fairness concepts while still being mindful of relationship balance over time.

4. Develop conflict resolution protocols

Every relationship experiences conflict. What distinguishes sustainable connections is not the absence of conflict but the capacity to move through it constructively.

Strong apocalypse crews develop:

- Shared vocabulary for discussing tensions
- Agreed-upon time-out signals when emotions get too intense
- Commitment to repair after ruptures
- Regular maintenance conversations that address small issues before they become large
- Appreciation for the growth that can come through working through disagreements

Having these protocols in place before major crises hit makes navigating the inevitable relationship challenges of apocalyptic times much more manageable.

5. Celebrate and appreciate consistently

Research consistently shows that relationships thrive with a ratio of at least five positive interactions for every negative one. During difficult times, we must intentionally create positive connection points to maintain this balance.

Simple practices include:

- Beginning conversations by sharing genuine appreciations
- Celebrating small wins and milestones
- Acknowledging specific contributions rather than generic gratitude
- Creating rituals of affirmation and recognition
- Documenting good moments to revisit during harder times

These positive reinforcement practices prevent relationships from becoming defined solely by problem-solving during crises.

Building Resilience Through Relationship Diversity

While close, intimate connections form the core of most apocalypse crews, resilience research suggests that diverse relationship networks provide the most robust support during prolonged challenges.

Consider intentionally cultivating:

1. Age diversity

Intergenerational connections provide unique perspectives and resources. Older individuals often bring historical context and wisdom from previous challenges, while younger connections offer fresh approaches and technical skills relevant to current conditions.

2. Geographic diversity

While local connections are essential for immediate physical support, maintaining some relationships with people in different locations provides perspective, alternative information sources, and potential relocation resources if necessary.

3. Skill and resource diversity

An apocalypse crew where everyone has identical skills and resources contains significant vulnerabilities. Cultivating connections with people who bring different capacities—practical skills, emotional intelligence, access to different resource networks—creates more comprehensive collective resilience.

4. Worldview diversity (within bounds)

While fundamental values alignment remains important, some diversity of worldview within your crew strengthens collective sense-making. People from different cultural backgrounds, professional fields, or life experiences can help identify blind spots and expand possibility thinking.

5. Temperament diversity

A crew composed entirely of action-oriented pragmatists might lack emotional processing capacity. A crew of philosophical meaning-seekers might struggle with practical implementation. Temperament diversity creates balanced collective responses to challenges.

This diversity must exist within boundaries of mutual respect and shared foundational values. The goal isn't to surround yourself with people who fundamentally oppose your core principles, but to cultivate relationships with people who share your basic orientation while bringing different perspectives and capacities.

When You Can't Find Your Crew (Yet)

What if, despite your best efforts, you haven't yet found your apocalypse crew? What if geographic isolation, life circumstances, or social anxiety make connection difficult? What if previous relationship wounds make trust challenging?

First, know you're not alone in this struggle. The loneliness epidemic predates our current apocalyptic circumstances, and many people find themselves without adequate support networks.

Second, consider these bridging strategies:

1. Structured connection points

Sometimes direct "make friends" approaches feel overwhelming. Structured activities with built-in social components can be easier entry points:

- Volunteer opportunities with regular schedules
- Classes or workshops where you see the same people repeatedly
- Community gardens or shared projects with practical focus
- Digital communities with specific shared interests

These provide scaffolding for connection with reduced social pressure.

2. Professional support as a starting point

Therapists, coaches, community health workers, and other professionals can provide temporary support structures while you build broader connection networks. While these relationships have professional boundaries, they can offer genuine support and help you develop relationship skills for other contexts.

3. Literary connection

Books, podcasts, and other media created by people navigating similar challenges can provide a form of one-way connection that, while not reciprocal, still reduces isolation. Many people find that certain authors or content creators become "virtual mentors" during difficult periods.

4. Graduated vulnerability

If past relationship wounds make trust difficult, consider a gradual approach to connection— starting with lower-risk contexts and slowly building toward deeper relationships as evidence of trustworthiness accumulates.

5. Single-dimension connections

Sometimes we feel we need to find people who connect with all aspects of our experience. In reality, having different connections for different dimensions of life—perhaps an online community for one interest, a neighbor for practical support, a distant friend for emotional processing—can collectively provide significant support.

6. Relationship with self as foundation

While not replacing the need for external connection, developing a strong relationship with yourself provides essential resilience when external support is limited. Self-compassion practices, internal dialog work, and self-knowledge all strengthen this foundation.

Remember that crew-building is an ongoing process, not a one-time achievement. Many people find their most meaningful connections later in life, often after periods of significant loneliness. The effort to find your people, while sometimes discouraging, remains one of the most worthwhile investments in apocalyptic times.

The Emergency Contact

As we conclude this chapter, I want to emphasize one specific action item: identify your emergency contact person—the first person you'd call in a crisis, and who would call you in theirs.

Make this explicit. Have the conversation. Exchange relevant information (medications, allergies, important documents, digital passwords in case of incapacitation). Discuss scenarios and preferences.

Even if your full apocalypse crew is still under construction, having at least one clearly designated emergency contact person creates a critical safety line for navigating both personal and collective crises.

If you truly cannot identify a single person who could serve this role currently, make finding that person a top priority—even above building a broader network. One solid emergency contact relationship provides a foundation upon which other connections can develop.

In the next chapter, we'll explore specific daily practices that help maintain your resilience during apocalyptic times, building on the relationship foundation we've established here.

Remember: humans have survived every type of disaster through collective response. We are a cooperative species by nature. Finding your people isn't just a nice addition to apocalypse survival—it's the central strategy. No one survives alone. But together, our capacity for resilience is remarkable.

CHAPTER 6: Daily Rituals That Actually Help

Let's start with a confession: I hate morning routines. I despise productivity hacks. I roll my eyes at life optimization strategies. And if one more wellness influencer tells me that success is just a matter of drinking lemon water and journaling at 5 AM, I might throw my phone into the ocean.

In apocalyptic times, the standard self-help advice can feel not just tone-deaf but actively offensive. "Manifest abundance" while systems collapse? "Hustle harder" while working three jobs to afford rent? "Just meditate" while processing genuine trauma?

No, thank you.

And yet... some version of daily structure and ritual genuinely does help during difficult periods. Not because routines magically fix external problems, but because they provide internal anchors when everything else feels chaotic. The right daily practices—ones that actually match your needs, capacity, and circumstances—can meaningfully support your resilience.

The key phrase here is "actually help." Not what looks good on Instagram. Not what some CEO claims fueled their success. Not what worked for your friend or your therapist or some random podcast guest. But what actually helps YOU navigate your specific version of the apocalypse.

In this chapter, we'll explore daily rituals that research suggests can support wellbeing during challenging times. But more importantly, we'll discuss how to customize these practices to fit your real life—with all its constraints, complications, and unique contours.

Morning Routines for When You Can Barely Function

The wellness world loves elaborate morning routines. Meditation! Journaling! Exercise! Cold plunges! Superfood smoothies! All before checking email, of course.

For many of us, especially during difficult periods, these aspirational routines are so far removed from our reality that they create more shame than inspiration. If getting out of bed feels like a victory, a 90-minute morning optimization protocol isn't happening.

But having some kind of morning anchor—even an extremely minimal one—can provide stability when you're struggling. The key is making it so simple and accessible that you can do it even on your worst days.

The Micro Morning Ritual

What's the smallest morning ritual that might actually help? Research suggests that brief moments of intentionality can significantly impact our relationship with the day ahead. Here's a framework for creating a micro morning ritual:

1. **One moment of physical grounding** This could be as simple as:

- ○ Feeling your feet on the floor for three seconds after standing
- ○ Taking one deliberate breath
- ○ Splashing cold water on your face
- ○ Stretching a single body part
- ○ Touching something with an interesting texture

2. **One moment of day orientation** This might look like:

- ○ Naming one thing you need to do today
- ○ Identifying one thing you're concerned about
- ○ Acknowledging one thing you're looking forward to
- ○ Setting a single intention for the day's quality ("Today I'll try to notice moments of connection")
- ○ Deciding on one small act of self-care to include

That's it. Two moments. Thirty seconds total, if that's all you have. The purpose isn't transformation but orientation—creating the smallest possible thread of continuity and intentionality from one day to the next.

On days when you have more capacity, you might expand this to include other elements that support your wellbeing. But having a micro version ensures you can maintain some form of ritual even when you're at your most depleted.

Morning Media Boundaries

Perhaps more important than what you include in your morning routine is what you exclude—specifically, immediate exposure to input designed to trigger stress responses.

Many of us reach for our phones as the very first action upon waking, immediately flooding our brains with:

- News alerts about disasters
- Work emails demanding attention
- Social media comparing our reality to others' highlight reels
- Messages requiring immediate emotional processing

This isn't just a matter of digital discipline—it's neurological self-protection. Your brain is most vulnerable to stress imprinting right after waking. The input you receive in those first moments can set your nervous system's baseline for the entire day.

Consider creating a morning media boundary—a specific period (even if just 10 minutes) when you protect yourself from potentially triggering input. This doesn't have to involve elaborate digital detoxing. It could be as simple as:

- Keeping your phone outside the bedroom
- Using airplane mode overnight and keeping it on until after breakfast
- Checking only specific apps (like a meditation timer) before a certain time
- Having a "news can wait" policy until you've completed your micro ritual

If your life circumstances make this impossible (many jobs require immediate availability, many caregiving situations require constant alertness), consider the smallest possible boundary you could create:

- Looking out the window before looking at your phone
- Reading one paragraph of something inspiring before checking alerts
- Taking three breaths between waking and engaging with demands

Even tiny barriers between sleep and stimulation can create valuable cognitive space for setting your own emotional agenda rather than immediately reacting to external triggers.

Morning Needs Assessment

One of the most supportive morning practices isn't adding specific activities but simply checking in with yourself about what you actually need today. This becomes especially important during apocalyptic times when your capacity may fluctuate dramatically.

A quick morning needs assessment might include asking:

- How did I sleep? How is my energy today?
- What's my emotional state as I begin the day?
- What's my biggest concern or challenge today?
- What's one thing my body needs today?
- What's one thing my mind needs today?
- What's one thing my heart needs today?
- What's one adjustment I could make to my plans based on this assessment?

This isn't about elaborate self-analysis. It's about bringing conscious awareness to your current state so you can make small adjustments that support your actual needs rather than pushing through on autopilot.

On high-capacity days, your assessment might lead you to tackle something challenging. On lower-capacity days, it might help you identify what to postpone or where to ask for help. Either way, it's a practice of responding to your reality rather than imposing generic expectations.

The Unexpected Power of Extremely Boring Habits

The most effective daily rituals for apocalyptic times are often the most mundane. Not the Instagram-worthy ones, not the biohacking ones, but the basic maintenance ones that provide fundamental stability.

These extremely boring habits include:

1. Regular meals

Eating at somewhat consistent times helps regulate blood sugar, which directly impacts mood and cognitive function. This doesn't require elaborate meal prep or nutritional optimization— just some basic eating structure to prevent the energy crashes that make everything feel worse.

During particularly difficult periods, consider:

- Having ready-to-eat options for low-capacity days
- Creating the simplest possible default meals that require minimal decisions
- Eating before you're desperately hungry (which makes everything harder)
- Being flexible about content while maintaining some timing structure

2. Basic hygiene

When struggling, tasks like showering, brushing teeth, or changing clothes can feel simultaneously trivial and overwhelming. Yet these basic physical maintenance activities provide both practical benefits (preventing health issues) and psychological ones (maintaining a sense of dignity and continuity).

If full hygiene routines feel impossible:

- Identify your "non-negotiable minimum" (maybe just teeth brushing and face washing)
- Create easier versions for low-capacity days (wet wipes instead of showers)
- Link hygiene tasks to small rewards or pleasures

- Focus on how different your body feels after basic care, not on external standards

3. Sleep boundaries

Nothing impacts psychological resilience more directly than sleep. Creating even minimal boundaries around sleep timing and conditions can significantly affect your capacity to handle stress.

Realistic sleep boundaries might include:

- A "wind-down" signal to your brain (could be as simple as a specific sound or light adjustment)
- A rough target for when you'll at least begin the sleep process
- Some protection of your sleep space from stimulating activities
- A plan for sleep disruptions that includes comfort rather than just frustration

4. Movement minimums

Regular physical movement is one of the most evidence-supported interventions for both mental and physical health. This doesn't require intense workouts or special equipment—even very small movement breaks show benefits.

Accessible movement practices include:

- Standing and stretching briefly once per hour
- Walking for five minutes, even just around your living space
- Gentle range-of-motion movements for major joints
- Brief moments of slightly increased heart rate

5. Outdoor exposure

Regular contact with outdoor environments—even brief and urban ones—consistently shows benefits for mood regulation and stress reduction. The combination of natural light, broader visual horizons, and connection to more-than-human reality provides a valuable counterbalance to indoor screen-focused existence.

If extended nature time isn't accessible:

- Stand by a window with a view of sky for one minute
- Step outside your door briefly once per day
- Notice one natural element in your environment (a plant, the quality of light, air movement)
- Track the phase of the moon or seasonal changes in available plant life

These habits aren't glamorous. They won't transform your life or solve systemic problems. But they create a foundation of basic biological support that makes everything else more manageable.

During apocalyptic times, when external circumstances generate significant stress, creating this foundation becomes not a luxury but a necessity. Without it, even our best psychological and social resources become depleted more quickly.

Why Consistency Matters (Even When It's Pathetically Small)

Here's a paradox of human psychology: we simultaneously crave novelty and consistency. We need both change and stability. During chaotic times, the stability part of this equation becomes especially important.

Consistent rituals, even extremely small ones, provide several psychological benefits:

1. Reduced decision fatigue

Each decision we make depletes limited cognitive resources. Rituals convert choices into automatic behaviors, preserving mental energy for more important matters. When external circumstances demand constant adaptation, having some areas of life operate on autopilot becomes precious cognitive conservation.

2. Increased sense of agency

When much feels beyond our control, consistent daily practices remind us of our capacity to influence at least our immediate experience. This sense of agency—the feeling that our actions matter—is a core component of psychological resilience.

3. Temporal anchoring

Regular rituals create a sense of continuity through time, connecting yesterday to today to tomorrow. This temporal anchoring helps counter the "endless present" feeling that often accompanies crisis, where each day blurs indistinguishably into the next.

4. Baseline regulation

Consistent routines help regulate biological systems, from circadian rhythms to digestion to hormone production. This physiological regulation directly impacts emotional regulation capacity, creating more stable ground for navigating external chaos.

5. Identity reinforcement

The things we do consistently become part of our self-concept. Daily rituals that align with our values reinforce our sense of self during periods when external forces might otherwise fragment our identity.

The benefits of consistency come not from the specific content of rituals but from their regularity. This means that smaller, more sustainable rituals actually provide more benefit than elaborate ones performed sporadically.

Put another way: a two-minute daily practice you actually do creates more stability than a 30-minute "ideal" practice you rarely complete.

This perspective liberates us from perfectionism about daily rituals. The goal isn't Instagram-worthy morning routines or life-changing productivity systems. It's creating enough structure to support wellbeing while maintaining flexibility to adapt to changing circumstances.

Creating Ritual Scaffolding

How do we develop daily rituals that provide stability without becoming rigid expectations that create more stress when we inevitably fail to meet them? The answer lies in what I call "ritual scaffolding"—flexible structures that support rather than constrain.

The Modular Approach

Instead of seeing daily rituals as all-or-nothing routines, consider them modular systems with different levels you can engage depending on your capacity:

Level 1: Survival Mode The absolute minimum practices that provide basic support during your most depleted periods. These should be so simple you could do them during illness or extreme stress.

Level 2: Maintenance Mode The practices that help you maintain equilibrium during normal stress levels—not thriving perhaps, but steadily managing.

Level 3: Fortification Mode The expanded practices you engage when you have more capacity, building reserves for more challenging periods.

Having this modular approach prepared in advance allows you to flex between levels without feeling like you're failing. You're simply deploying the appropriate level of practice for your current capacity.

Trigger-Based Rather Than Time-Based

Another helpful approach is developing rituals tied to specific triggers rather than clock times. This works better for irregular schedules and fluctuating conditions.

Examples of trigger-based rituals:

- A brief centering practice before opening work communications (rather than at a specific time)
- A transition ritual between different life domains (work/home, online/offline)
- A reset practice after specific stressors (difficult interactions, upsetting news)
- A grounding ritual before challenging tasks or situations

These trigger-based practices create consistency through situational association rather than temporal rigidity, making them more adaptable to changing circumstances.

Anchoring to Existing Habits

New habits form more easily when connected to established ones. Consider linking new supportive practices to behaviors already firmly embedded in your routine:

- Brief breathing practice while waiting for coffee to brew
- Gratitude moment while brushing teeth
- Body scan while showering
- Intention setting while putting on shoes
- Media boundary while using the bathroom first thing in morning

These "habit stacks" leverage existing neural pathways, making new practices feel like natural extensions of your current routine rather than foreign impositions.

Tracking Without Tyranny

Some form of ritual tracking can support consistency, but traditional "don't break the chain" approaches often create unnecessary pressure. Consider more flexible tracking methods:

- Noting which module level (survival, maintenance, fortification) you're operating at each day
- Tracking overall engagement patterns without requiring daily perfection

- Celebrating adaptation rather than just consistency ("I adjusted my practice to fit difficult circumstances")
- Using tracking as information rather than evaluation ("Interesting that I've been in survival mode for two weeks—what might that indicate?")

The goal of tracking isn't to enforce rigid compliance but to increase self-awareness and identify patterns that might inform adjustments.

Daily Ritual Design Workshop

Let's put these principles into practice by designing daily rituals specifically for apocalyptic times. This isn't a prescription but a framework for creating practices that actually match your life.

Step 1: Identify your key support needs

What specifically helps you function during difficult periods? Common areas include:

- Energy regulation (managing fatigue/ overwhelm)
- Emotional processing (handling difficult feelings)
- Cognitive space (mental clarity amid chaos)
- Physical wellbeing (basic bodily needs)

- Connection (maintaining important relationships)
- Meaning (finding purpose amid difficulty)

For each area, note specific practices that have genuinely helped in the past—not what you think should help, but what actually has.

Step 2: Create your modular system

For each key support area, define what practices would look like at different capacity levels:

Survival Mode Example:

- Energy: One 5-minute outdoor pause
- Emotional: Name feelings out loud once daily
- Cognitive: 30 seconds of eyes closed between tasks
- Physical: Minimum hygiene plus one glass of water with each meal
- Connection: Text one person
- Meaning: Notice one thing that matters to you

Maintenance Mode Example:

- Energy: Morning/afternoon outdoor breaks plus one boundary around energy-draining activities

- Emotional: Brief journaling or voice memo emotional check-in
- Cognitive: Two scheduled "no input" periods daily
- Physical: Regular meals, basic movement, consistent sleep start time
- Connection: One meaningful interaction plus regular check-ins with core people
- Meaning: Small actions aligned with key values

Fortification Mode Example:

- Energy: Proactive rest periods, nature time, energy-generating activities
- Emotional: Extended processing through conversation or creative expression
- Cognitive: Longer reflection periods, learning engagement, idea exploration
- Physical: More intentional movement, meal planning, sleep optimization
- Connection: Deeper conversations, group engagement, support offering
- Meaning: Larger projects connected to purpose, contribution activities

Step 3: Identify implementation triggers

For each practice, decide what will prompt you to engage it:

- Time-based triggers (upon waking, before sleep)
- Activity transitions (before/after work, entering/leaving home)
- Response triggers (after exposure to disturbing news, before difficult conversations)
- Physical cues (hunger, fatigue, tension)
- Emotional states (anxiety, overwhelm, numbness)

Step 4: Create environmental supports

How can you adjust your environment to make these practices more accessible?

- Visual reminders in key locations
- Necessary materials prepared and visible
- Digital settings that support your intentions
- Physical spaces designated for specific practices
- Removal of barriers to desired behaviors

Step 5: Establish flexible accountability

How will you track engagement without creating additional stress?

- Simple notation systems
- Regular self-check-ins
- Supportive external accountability

- Periodic review and adjustment
- Celebration of adaptation and resilience

Step 6: Plan for disruption

How will you respond when (not if) your rituals get disrupted?

- Re-entry practices after disruption
- Simplified versions for unusual circumstances
- Permission statements for necessary adaptations
- Recovery protocols for extended disruptions

Remember: The goal of daily rituals during apocalyptic times isn't self-optimization or performance enhancement. It's creating enough internal stability to navigate external chaos with resilience. The "success" metric isn't perfect adherence but whether the practices actually support your wellbeing in tangible ways.

Beyond Individual Practice: Collective Rituals

While personal daily rituals provide crucial support, collective rituals offer additional benefits particularly valuable during apocalyptic times. Consider incorporating some form of shared practice into your regular rhythm.

Collective rituals might include:

1. Regular connections with specific others

- Daily check-ins with household members
- Weekly calls with distant loved ones
- Monthly gatherings with wider community
- Seasonal celebrations with extended networks

These connection points create interpersonal continuity that complements personal practice.

2. Normalized collective emotional processing

- Sharing circles where feelings are acknowledged
- Grief rituals that honor losses
- Anger expression in controlled settings
- Joy and pleasure celebrations that counterbalance difficulty

These shared emotional practices prevent isolation in difficult feelings.

3. Meaning-oriented gatherings

- Discussion groups exploring larger questions

- Action circles focused on response to challenges
- Learning communities developing new skills
- Creative collaborations making beauty amid difficulty

These purpose-focused gatherings connect personal experience to larger contexts.

4. Resource sharing systems

- Meal exchanges that reduce individual burden
- Childcare rotations that distribute caregiving
- Skill shares that leverage diverse capacities
- Tool libraries that increase collective access

These mutual aid practices convert individual vulnerability into collective resilience.

5. Rest and celebration containers

- Sabbath-like periods of collective pause
- Milestone acknowledgments that mark time
- Pleasure-centered gatherings that permit joy amid struggle
- Play spaces that allow temporary liberation from responsibility

These rejuvenation practices prevent collective burnout and sustain long-term engagement.

Participation in collective rituals doesn't require elaborate community structures. It can begin with just one other person, a small online group, or occasional in-person gatherings. The key is some form of regular shared practice that embeds individual experience within wider connection.

The Anti-Productivity Perspective

As we conclude this exploration of daily rituals, I want to explicitly counter the productivity-centered approach that dominates much habit and routine discourse.

The rituals we've discussed aren't about becoming more productive, more successful, or more optimized. They're about becoming more sustainable, more present, and more connected to what matters most during difficult times.

This anti-productivity perspective recognizes that:

- The goal of daily practice isn't increasing output but sustaining presence
- Rest isn't recovery for more work but a legitimate state in itself
- Consistency matters for wellbeing, not performance metrics

- Different capacity levels require different expectations
- Functioning is often victory enough in apocalyptic times

In a culture obsessed with optimization, choosing rituals based on genuine support rather than productivity enhancement becomes a radical act. It asserts that your worth isn't tied to your output. It creates space for being rather than just doing. It acknowledges human limits in systems that prefer to ignore them.

This perspective doesn't diminish the importance of daily rituals but transforms their purpose from self-improvement to self-sustenance. Not becoming better, but continuing. Not optimizing, but enduring. Not transcending human limits, but honoring them.

As writer and activist adrienne maree brown notes: "How we are at the small scale is how we are at the large scale." The daily rituals we practice aren't separate from our larger response to apocalyptic circumstances—they're microcosms of it.

When we create daily practices that honor our actual needs, capacities, and humanity rather than pushing toward impossible ideals, we begin embodying the very values needed for more sustainable collective futures: respect for limits, prioritization of care, balance of structure and flexibility, integration of rest and action.

In this light, the seemingly small choice of how you begin your day becomes not trivial but profound—a tiny but significant vote for the kind of world you wish to create. Not through grand gestures, but through the revolutionary ordinary practices that acknowledge what humans actually need to thrive.

This doesn't mean your morning routine will save the world. It won't. But it might help you show up more fully to participate in the collective work of navigating these challenging times. And that showing up—day after day, in ways that honor both your capacity and your values—is no small thing.

In the next chapter, we'll explore how these daily foundations support larger explorations of meaning and purpose amid apocalyptic circumstances— how the "horizontal" dimension of daily practice connects to the "vertical" dimension of transcendent purpose.

PART III: FINDING JOY IN THE FLAMES

CHAPTER 7: The Science of Happiness During Hard Times

Is it even possible to experience genuine happiness while the world burns around us? Is joy during apocalyptic times a form of denial, a psychological defense mechanism, or perhaps even a moral failure in the face of widespread suffering?

These aren't just philosophical questions. They're deeply personal ones that many of us grapple with daily. The guilt that accompanies moments of pleasure while others suffer. The confusion of feeling both despair and delight in the same day—sometimes the same hour. The uncertainty about whether pursuing joy amid crisis is appropriate or oblivious.

Let's start with what the research actually tells us about happiness during difficult times—not the Instagram inspirational quote version, but the evidence-based understanding of how human beings experience and maintain wellbeing even in challenging circumstances.

What Research Actually Says About Resilience (Without the Bullshit)

The past few decades have seen an explosion of research on psychological resilience—the capacity to maintain or regain wellbeing despite adversity. This research offers important insights, but it's often misrepresented in popular culture in ways that create unrealistic expectations.

Here's what the science actually shows:

1. Resilience is common, not exceptional

Much early resilience research focused on "extraordinary" individuals who thrived despite extreme adversity, creating the impression that resilience requires special qualities or rare strength.

More recent research reveals that resilience is actually the most common response to adversity. In a landmark study following New Yorkers after the 9/11 attacks, researchers George Bonanno and colleagues found that about 65% of people maintained relatively stable psychological functioning. Similar patterns appear in studies of natural disasters, war zones, and personal tragedies.

This doesn't mean most people don't struggle or experience suffering—they absolutely do. But it does mean that maintaining basic functioning and experiencing moments of positive emotion alongside distress is normal, not exceptional.

The practical implication? If you're having moments of joy or normality amid crisis, you're not weird or insensitive. You're demonstrating typical human resilience.

2. Resilience fluctuates rather than remains constant

Another popular misconception portrays resilience as a fixed trait—something you either have or don't have. Research clearly shows that resilience fluctuates based on:

- Current resource availability (sleep, support, financial stability)
- Cumulative stress burden (how many simultaneous challenges you're facing)
- Life stage and developmental factors
- Health status (physical and mental)
- Social context and cultural factors

This means you might demonstrate remarkable resilience during one crisis yet struggle significantly during another. Or you might handle the early stages of a prolonged challenge well but find your capacity diminishing over time as resources deplete.

The practical implication? Judging yourself for struggling now when you "handled things better before" misunderstands how resilience actually works. Different circumstances require different responses, and resilience capacity naturally fluctuates.

3. Multiple resilience pathways exist

Pop psychology often prescribes singular paths to resilience: "Just practice gratitude!" "Meditate daily!" "Focus on what you can control!"

Research shows multiple, equally valid pathways to maintained wellbeing during adversity:

- Social connection and support seeking
- Meaning-making and purpose orientation
- Problem-solving and practical action
- Emotional processing and expression
- Cognitive flexibility and reframing
- Physiological regulation practices
- Spiritual and existential approaches

Different approaches work better for different people, different types of adversity, and different contexts. What supports one person's resilience might actively hinder another's.

The practical implication? There's no single "right way" to navigate hard times. Finding approaches that match your specific needs, values, and circumstances matters more than following generic resilience prescriptions.

4. Resilience coexists with suffering

Perhaps the most harmful resilience myth suggests that truly resilient people don't experience negative emotions or significant distress. This creates the impression that if you're struggling emotionally, you're somehow failing at resilience.

Research consistently shows that resilience isn't the absence of suffering but the capacity to experience difficult emotions while still maintaining:

- Some emotional flexibility (not getting permanently stuck in one state)
- Periods of positive emotion alongside distress
- Connection to meaning and purpose
- Basic functioning in important life domains
- The ability to access support when needed

True resilience isn't about not feeling bad; it's about not being defined or completely incapacitated by difficult feelings.

The practical implication? Your painful emotions don't indicate failed resilience. They're normal responses to abnormal circumstances, and can coexist with moments of joy, purpose, and connection.

5. Resilience depends on systems, not just individuals

The most pernicious resilience myth frames it as purely individual—suggesting that your ability to withstand adversity depends solely on personal qualities rather than systemic factors.

Research clearly demonstrates that resilience depends significantly on:

- Material resource access (financial stability, healthcare, safe housing)
- Community support structures
- Cultural context and collective narratives
- Institutional responsiveness to needs
- Historical patterns of resource distribution
- Environmental conditions

Individual practices matter, but they operate within these larger contexts that significantly constrain or expand resilience capacity.

The practical implication? If you're struggling, it's not simply a personal failure of resilience. Systemic factors genuinely impact your ability to maintain wellbeing during adversity, and acknowledging these realities isn't making excuses—it's accepting an evidence-based understanding of how resilience actually works.

Why Your Brain Needs Joy to Function During Crisis

Beyond dismantling resilience myths, research offers important insights about why positive emotions aren't just pleasant but functionally necessary during crisis periods.

The Broaden-and-Build Theory

Psychologist Barbara Fredrickson's influential "broaden-and-build" theory explains that positive emotions serve specific adaptive functions during stress:

1. **Cognitive broadening:** Positive emotions temporarily expand our attention and thinking, helping us see more possibilities and connections. This counters the narrowing effect of chronic stress, which creates tunnel vision focused only on threats.

2. **Resource building:** Positive emotional experiences help build personal resources—new skills, stronger relationships, fresh insights—that become available during future challenges.

3. **Undoing negative arousal:** Positive emotions help physiologically "undo" the effects of negative emotional arousal,

allowing stress response systems to reset rather than remain chronically activated.

This research suggests that experiencing joy, curiosity, awe, or other positive emotions during crisis isn't frivolous—it's biologically adaptive, helping maintain the cognitive flexibility and physiological regulation needed to respond effectively to challenges.

The Parasympathetic Necessity

Our nervous systems have two primary branches: the sympathetic (activation/fight-flight-freeze) and parasympathetic (rest-digest-connect). Both are essential for survival, but under chronic stress, many people get stuck in sympathetic dominance.

Research shows that parasympathetic activation—which generates feelings of safety, connection, and pleasure—is necessary for:

- Immune system functioning
- Digestive processes
- Cellular repair and regeneration
- Memory consolidation
- Executive function and decision-making
- Social engagement capabilities

Without regular parasympathetic activation, these essential functions become impaired, reducing both immediate coping capacity and long-term health. Activities that generate positive emotions help activate this parasympathetic response, essentially performing necessary maintenance on biological systems.

Hedonic Adaptation and Crisis

Humans demonstrate remarkable hedonic adaptation—the tendency to return to baseline happiness levels despite changed circumstances, both positive and negative. Research on how this functions during crisis reveals interesting patterns:

- While immediate happiness drops during adverse events, most people experience significant hedonic adaptation even to severe ongoing challenges
- This adaptation isn't denial but a natural psychological process that prevents emotional overwhelm
- Preventing adaptation through constant crisis focus can create unnecessary suffering beyond what the situation itself generates
- Allowing natural hedonic adaptation (returning to moments of normalcy and pleasure) typically improves rather than impairs effective crisis response

This research suggests that experiencing joy during apocalyptic times isn't a failure to grasp severity but a natural psychological mechanism that prevents emotional system overload.

Affect Balance and Functioning

Contrary to the idea that crisis requires exclusive focus on negative realities, research on "affect balance" (the ratio of positive to negative emotions) shows that maintaining some positive emotional experiences alongside negative ones optimizes functioning during stress.

Studies suggest:

- A ratio of approximately 3:1 positive to negative emotions supports optimal cognitive flexibility and problem-solving
- Exclusive focus on negative information actually impairs effective threat response
- Some positive emotional experiences improve information processing, decision-making, and social coordination during crisis
- Even brief positive emotions can create "psychological time-outs" that prevent emotional exhaustion

This doesn't mean artificially manufacturing positivity or denying negative realities. It means allowing natural moments of positive emotion to occur alongside the difficult feelings that crises generate.

How Pleasure and Pain Coexist (And Why That's Normal)

Perhaps the most important scientific insight about happiness during hard times is that pleasure and pain aren't opposite ends of a single spectrum. They're separate, parallel experiences that can and do coexist.

The Two-Channel Model of Emotion

Psychological research has increasingly moved away from viewing emotions as a single pleasure-pain continuum toward understanding them as operating on at least two separate channels:

- The negative affect channel (threat, loss, harm)
- The positive affect channel (reward, connection, interest)

These channels can be simultaneously activated, creating complex emotional states where joy and sorrow, connection and grief, interest and fear coexist.

This explains common but seemingly contradictory experiences like:

- Laughing at a funeral while genuinely grieving
- Feeling both anxious and excited before an important event
- Experiencing beauty and horror simultaneously in crisis situations
- Finding intimate connection during collective tragedy

These aren't emotional malfunctions but normal operations of our parallel emotional processing systems.

The Mixed-Emotion Advantage

Interestingly, research suggests that experiencing mixed emotions (simultaneous positive and negative feelings) during adversity may actually support resilience better than either pure positivity or pure negativity.

Studies show mixed emotional states can:

- Prevent emotional extremes that impair functioning

- Create psychological complexity that supports meaning-making
- Improve emotional differentiation and regulation
- Better reflect the true complexity of difficult situations

This suggests that allowing ourselves to experience joy alongside sorrow during apocalyptic times isn't emotional confusion but emotional sophistication.

Emotional Granularity and Crisis Coping

Related research on "emotional granularity"—the ability to distinguish between specific emotional states rather than experiencing vague "good" or "bad" feelings—shows that more granular emotional experience improves crisis coping.

People who can differentiate between specific positive emotions (joy vs. contentment vs. awe vs. interest) and specific negative emotions (anxiety vs. anger vs. sadness vs. disappointment) demonstrate:

- More flexible coping strategies
- Better emotion regulation

- Improved interpersonal functioning during stress
- Greater resilience to trauma's psychological impacts

This suggests that developing a more nuanced understanding of our emotional experiences—including the specific positive emotions that remain possible during crisis—supports rather than undermines effective coping.

The Happiness Traps to Avoid During Crisis

While research clearly shows that happiness during hard times is both possible and functional, certain approaches to pursuing happiness during crisis can backfire dramatically. Here are the most common happiness traps to avoid:

1. Toxic Positivity

Forcing artificial positive thinking while suppressing or denying genuine negative emotions creates what psychologists call "experiential avoidance"—a pattern associated with worse psychological outcomes during crisis.

Signs of toxic positivity include:

- Shaming negative emotions ("Just be grateful!")
- Using positive statements to shut down authentic expression
- Minimizing genuine problems with platitudes
- Treating positive thinking as moral superiority
- Suggesting happiness is simply a choice regardless of circumstances

Research consistently shows this approach impairs rather than supports resilience, creating additional suffering beyond what the crisis itself generates.

2. Hedonic Treadmill Acceleration

Another happiness trap involves constantly seeking new, more intense pleasurable experiences to counteract crisis-related negative emotions. This "hedonic treadmill acceleration" creates diminishing returns as:

- Sensation thresholds increase, requiring ever-stronger stimuli
- Novel experiences become normalized more quickly
- Contrast effects make return to everyday life more difficult
- Resources deplete faster than they can be replenished

This pattern often manifests as increased consumption (shopping, substances, entertainment, food) that provides momentary distraction but ultimately depletes rather than restores resources.

3. Comparative Happiness

During crisis, many people fall into patterns of comparative happiness judgments:

- "I shouldn't complain when others have it worse"
- "At least I'm not as affected as those people"
- "I should be handling this better like so-and-so"

These comparisons create artificial happiness hierarchies that invalidate authentic emotional experience and create additional shame on top of crisis-related suffering.

Research shows that allowing direct emotional experience without comparative judgments actually improves crisis coping, even when those emotions are difficult.

4. Achievement-Based Happiness

Crisis often disrupts normal achievement patterns, making achievement-dependent happiness particularly vulnerable. People who primarily derive happiness from productivity, accomplishment, and external validation tend to struggle more during circumstances that limit these opportunities.

Developing non-achievement sources of positive emotion—simple pleasures, connection, curiosity, appreciation—creates more sustainable happiness pathways during disruption.

5. Future-Conditional Happiness

Perhaps the most subtle happiness trap during ongoing crisis is the "when this is over" mentality—placing happiness exclusively in a hypothetical future when current challenges have passed.

While hope for better circumstances is important, research shows that indefinitely postponing positive emotional experience creates:

- Hedonic deficits that impair current functioning
- Psychological rigidity that reduces adaptive capacity
- Difficulty recognizing improvements that don't match imagined ideals
- Lost opportunities for meaningful experience amid crisis

Learning to find moments of genuine joy within current constraints, rather than making all happiness conditional on future resolution, supports both immediate wellbeing and long-term resilience.

Evidence-Based Happiness Practices for Apocalyptic Times

So what does the research suggest actually works for maintaining genuine happiness during hard times? Here are evidence-supported approaches that avoid the common traps while creating sustainable positive emotional experiences amid crisis:

1. Savoring and Appreciation

Research consistently shows that brief but intentional engagement with positive experiences —a practice called "savoring"—generates disproportionate wellbeing benefits during stressful periods.

Effective savoring involves:

- Slowing down to notice pleasurable sensory experiences

- Consciously directing attention to what's enjoyable about an experience
- Briefly acknowledging that this positive moment exists alongside difficulties
- Allowing the experience to be felt in the body, not just noted intellectually

Unlike forced gratitude, which can become another "should," natural appreciation emerges from direct experience of what genuinely feels good or meaningful, however small.

2. Relational Connection

No factor predicts crisis resilience more consistently than relational connection. The positive emotions generated through authentic human connection provide unique benefits that individual coping strategies cannot replicate.

Research-supported approaches include:

- Brief but present-focused interactions that involve genuine disclosure
- Shared experience of both difficulties and pleasures
- Perceived understanding rather than advice-giving
- Mutual aid that creates reciprocity rather than dependency

- Collective meaning-making about shared challenges

These connections need not be elaborate—even brief exchanges of authentic recognition create significant positive emotion that buffers stress effects.

3. Flow and Engagement

Psychologist Mihaly Csikszentmihalyi's research on "flow"—the state of absorbed engagement in optimally challenging activities—shows that flow experiences generate positive emotions even in extremely adverse circumstances, from prison camps to disaster zones.

Flow-supporting activities typically involve:

- Clear goals with immediate feedback
- Balance between challenge and skill
- Deep concentration that temporarily suspends self-consciousness
- Sense of control and competence
- Intrinsic reward rather than external validation

During apocalyptic times, activities that create flow states provide psychological respite that allows emotional resources to replenish.

4. Meaning Orientation

Research from multiple traditions confirms that connecting individual experience to larger meaning frameworks significantly supports wellbeing during adversity. This can include:

- Contribution to others' welfare
- Connection to transcendent values or spiritual traditions
- Participation in collective efforts addressing challenges
- Creation of beauty or knowledge
- Preservation of important cultural or natural elements
- Bearing witness to significant events

Unlike toxic positivity, meaning orientation doesn't deny difficulty but integrates it into narratives that maintain purpose and agency amid constraints.

5. Physiological Regulation

Perhaps most basic but often overlooked are practices that directly regulate the body's stress response systems, creating the physiological conditions where positive emotions become possible:

- Brief cardiovascular exercise
- Nature exposure

- Adequate sleep
- Social touch (with consent)
- Breath regulation
- Rhythm and movement
- Sensory pleasure

These approaches work bottom-up, directly shifting physiological states that influence emotional experience, rather than trying to think our way into feeling better.

6. Balanced Awareness

Research on "balanced awareness" during crisis shows benefits from approaches that:

- Acknowledge difficulties without fixating exclusively on them
- Allow attention to move naturally between challenges and resources
- Create boundaries around crisis-related input
- Include regular exposure to non-crisis content and experiences
- Maintain awareness of what remains intact alongside what's threatened

This balanced awareness isn't denial but attentional discipline that prevents crisis-narrowing without ignoring important realities.

7. Self-Compassion

No happiness practice for apocalyptic times would be complete without self-compassion—the orientation toward one's own suffering with kindness rather than judgment. Research by Kristin Neff and others shows that self-compassion:

- Reduces rumination and persistent negative affect
- Improves physiological recovery from stress
- Enhances motivation for self-care and sustainable action
- Supports connection rather than isolation during difficulty
- Provides psychological safety necessary for authentic positive emotion

Self-compassion isn't self-pity or self-indulgence but a stable base of self-kindness that allows both honestly facing difficulties and genuinely experiencing available joys.

A Personalized Approach to Crisis Happiness

Perhaps the most important scientific insight about happiness during hard times is that no universal formula exists. The practices that genuinely support your wellbeing depend on:

- Your unique neurophysiology and temperament
- Your specific values and meaning frameworks
- Your particular crisis circumstances and constraints
- Your available resources (internal and external)
- Your cultural context and community support

This means developing a personalized approach based on self-knowledge rather than following generic happiness prescriptions.

Some questions to guide this exploration:

- What specific positive emotions remain most accessible to you during difficulty? (Joy, interest, awe, contentment, amusement, love, etc.)
- What activities reliably generate these emotions for you personally?
- What approaches help you maintain emotional equilibrium during stress?
- What happiness practices feel authentic rather than forced given your values?
- What has historically helped you navigate difficult periods?

The goal isn't maximizing happiness during apocalyptic times—an impossible and potentially harmful standard—but finding sustainable sources of genuine positive emotion that coexist with honest acknowledgment of challenges.

The Moral Dimension of Crisis Happiness

Before concluding this exploration of happiness science, we must address the moral question many people grapple with: Is it right to experience joy while others suffer? Does happiness during apocalyptic times reflect privilege, denial, or selfishness?

Research on collective trauma and moral injury offers important perspectives:

1. **Happiness as resource rather than indulgence**

Positive emotional experiences aren't just personal pleasures but resources that maintain the capacity for continued engagement with difficult realities. The positive emotions you experience aren't taken from others but rather sustain your ability to respond effectively to collective challenges.

2. False dichotomy of caring and joy

Research shows that people who maintain access to positive emotions alongside distress typically demonstrate greater rather than less capacity for empathy, prosocial behavior, and sustained engagement with challenging issues. Happiness and caring are complements, not competitors.

3. Witnessing the full spectrum

In disaster zones and conflict areas, researchers observe that authentic witnessing includes recognizing not just suffering but also the remarkable human capacity for joy, connection, and meaning amid adversity. Acknowledging the full spectrum of experience honors rather than diminishes others' reality.

4. The contagion effect

Emotional states are inherently contagious. Your sustainable happiness practices don't just benefit you but create ripple effects that influence others' emotional regulation capacity. This makes maintaining your own wellbeing an act of social responsibility rather than selfishness.

5. The testimony of survivors

Perhaps most compelling are consistent reports from survivors of extreme adversity—from concentration camps to natural disasters—who affirm that small moments of joy, beauty, and connection amid suffering weren't trivial but essential to both survival and human dignity.

The moral question shifts from "Is it okay to experience happiness during apocalyptic times?" to "How can I experience happiness in ways that support rather than detract from collective wellbeing?"

Conclusion: Joy as Sustenance, Not Escape

The science of happiness during hard times doesn't offer magical solutions or promises of perpetual positivity amid crisis. What it does provide is evidence-based understanding of how positive emotions function alongside difficulty—not as escape or denial but as necessary psychological sustenance for the journey.

The research tells us that:

- Joy amid hardship is normal, not exceptional
- Positive emotions serve functional purposes during crisis

- Multiple, equally valid pathways to maintained wellbeing exist
- Authentic happiness coexists with rather than replaces honest acknowledgment of difficulty
- Sustainable positive emotional experience supports rather than impairs effective crisis response

In the chapters ahead, we'll explore specific practices that build on these scientific insights—approaches to finding meaning, maintaining perspective, and creating moments of genuine joy even as the world burns around us. Not because we're ignoring the flames, but because these experiences give us the strength to face them.

As Holocaust survivor Viktor Frankl observed: "Between stimulus and response there is a space. In that space is our power to choose our response." The science of happiness during hard times helps us understand how to use that space wisely—to choose responses that honor both the reality of suffering and the human capacity for joy that somehow, remarkably, persists alongside it.

CHAPTER 8: Radical Enjoyment as Resistance

In times of crisis, we're often told explicitly or implicitly that enjoyment is frivolous, inappropriate, or selfish. That the only acceptable responses to apocalyptic circumstances are anxiety, grief, rage, or solemn productivity. That pleasure during difficult times reflects either privilege or denial.

But what if enjoyment during apocalyptic times isn't just psychologically beneficial, as we explored in the previous chapter, but politically significant? What if finding moments of joy and pleasure isn't retreating from reality but actively resisting systems that benefit from your despair?

In this chapter, we'll explore the radical potential of enjoyment as resistance—not as a replacement for other forms of action, but as a necessary complement that keeps those actions sustainable and authentic.

Why Enjoying Your Life Is a Political Act

To understand why enjoyment can be politically significant, we first need to recognize what dominant systems gain from your chronic distress:

1. Despair creates compliance

When people feel overwhelmed, hopeless, and exhausted, they're less likely to challenge existing power structures. Despair whispers, "Nothing will change anyway, so why try?" This psychological state benefits systems that want to avoid disruption.

Studies of authoritarian regimes consistently show that fostering public despair—often through unpredictable enforcement, constantly shifting narratives, and overwhelming information environments—is a core control strategy. It's not a conspiracy; it's a documented pattern of how power maintains itself.

In less extreme contexts, corporate and political systems still benefit when overwhelmed citizens and consumers:

- Accept deteriorating conditions as inevitable
- Feel too depleted to demand accountability
- Believe individual action is futile
- See no alternatives to current arrangements

When you refuse despair and maintain your capacity for joy, you preserve the psychological resources necessary for imagining and creating alternatives.

2. Distraction enables exploitation

While despair creates passive compliance, constant distraction creates active misdirection, keeping attention focused on manufactured emergencies, celebrity dramas, partisan outrage cycles, and identity conflicts rather than underlying systems.

Media ecosystems profit directly from your anxiety, outrage, and fear—emotions that increase engagement metrics but deplete your capacity for sustained attention to complex issues. The business model depends on keeping you in states of high arousal and low agency.

When you intentionally create space for genuine enjoyment rather than anxious distraction, you reclaim attentional resources that can be directed toward what actually matters to you.

3. Exhaustion prevents collective action

Systems of exploitation benefit when potential challengers are too exhausted for effective organization. When basic survival consumes all available energy, coordinated resistance becomes nearly impossible.

This exhaustion isn't just physical but emotional—the depletion that comes from constant outrage, perpetual crisis response, and the emotional labor of navigating increasingly precarious conditions.

When you preserve your capacity for joy and pleasure, you maintain energetic resources that can sustain long-term collective action rather than just reactive crisis response.

4. Isolation undermines solidarity

Perhaps most important, systems of domination thrive when people are isolated—not just physically but emotionally. When suffering feels entirely personal and disconnection becomes the norm, building the relationships necessary for collective power becomes increasingly difficult.

Joy, play, celebration, and pleasure have historically created spaces where people connect beyond utilitarian purposes—where they experience direct solidarity that can later support organized action.

When you create or participate in spaces of genuine enjoyment, you help maintain the relational infrastructure necessary for effective collective response to crisis.

In these ways, maintaining your capacity for enjoyment during apocalyptic times isn't escapism —it's preservation of exactly the psychological, attentional, energetic, and relational resources that transformative action requires.

Historical Examples of Joy as Resistance

This isn't just abstract theory. Throughout history, communities facing extreme oppression and crisis have recognized joyful practices as essential components of resistance:

Civil Rights Movement and the Freedom Songs

The American Civil Rights Movement incorporated music, dance, communal meals, and celebration alongside direct action, legal challenges, and economic boycotts. These weren't separate from "serious" activism but integral to maintaining movement resilience.

As historian and activist Vincent Harding noted: "The songs of the movement...were the way we talked to each other, the way we strengthened each other, the way we expressed our determination, our faith, and our courage. And all of these were affirmed in the midst of danger."

Freedom songs weren't just tactical tools but expressions of the joy and freedom being fought for—embodiments of the world being created rather than just protests against the world being rejected.

ACT UP and Radical Celebration

During the AIDS crisis, when government neglect and social stigma compounded medical trauma, organizations like ACT UP integrated direct action protests with dance parties, drag performances, and sexual celebration.

Activist Douglas Crimp's influential 1989 essay "Mourning and Militancy" argued explicitly against the false separation of grief from joy, pleasure from protest. As he wrote: "Militancy might arise from the need to mourn, need to find beauty within the crisis of AIDS."

These activists recognized that defending queer joy and sexual pleasure wasn't separate from fighting for medical research and treatment access —it was part of the same struggle against systems that deemed queer lives unworthy of either pleasure or preservation.

Indigenous Resistance Through Cultural Celebration

Indigenous communities facing genocidal policies have consistently maintained ceremonial practices, languages, art forms, and celebrations as core resistance strategies—recognizing that cultural joy directly counters colonial logics of elimination.

As Nick Estes of the Lower Brule Sioux Tribe writes: "Our ceremonies are revolutionary...Indigenous joy is revolutionary against the backdrop of a society that expects our devastation."

These practices aren't separate from more visible resistance tactics like land defense but part of an integrated approach that preserves exactly what colonization attempts to destroy—cultural continuity and collective joy that affirm Indigenous futures.

Prison Abolition and the Defense of Pleasure

Contemporary prison abolition movements explicitly link the defense of pleasure to the fight against carceral systems. Organizations like Survived & Punished and Critical Resistance reject the division between "deserving" and "undeserving" targets of state violence, defending the right to joy and pleasure for all people.

As activist Adrienne Maree Brown writes in Pleasure Activism: "I believe that by transforming our relationship to pleasure, we can create more space for joy, wholeness, and satisfaction in our lives as people trying to move social justice work forward."

These movements recognize that who is allowed pleasure and on what terms remains a deeply political question, with marginalized people's joy and pleasure historically subject to criminalization, pathologization, and violent suppression.

In all these cases, joy and pleasure weren't frivolous additions to "real" resistance but integral dimensions of challenging systems designed to exhaust, isolate, and demoralize those who oppose them.

Finding Beauty in Breakdown

Beyond its political implications, finding joy amid crisis often involves a particular skill: the ability to recognize beauty within breakdown—not as denial of difficulty but as expanded perception that holds both reality's pain and its persistent wonder.

This capacity has been explored across philosophical, spiritual, and artistic traditions:

The Japanese aesthetic of wabi-sabi

This traditional Japanese worldview finds beauty specifically in impermanence, imperfection, and incompleteness. Rather than seeing decay as merely tragic, wabi-sabi appreciates the particular beauty of things in transition—the weathered wood, the cracked ceramic, the fading flower.

Applied to apocalyptic times, this perspective invites us to notice not just what's being lost but what particular beauty emerges specifically through processes of change and dissolution.

Rebecca Solnit's "disaster communities"

In her book A Paradise Built in Hell, Rebecca Solnit documents how disasters often generate remarkable moments of community, purpose, and even joy amid suffering—not despite the breakdown of normal conditions but because of it.

As temporary suspensions of ordinary social divisions, disasters can create openings for connection and meaning that conventional structures often inhibit. Recognizing these emergent possibilities isn't denying disaster's harm but perceiving its complex totality.

Emergent beauty in ecological succession

Ecologists studying disturbed landscapes—after fires, floods, or human damage—observe that while initial destruction is real, these disturbances also create conditions for new forms of beauty through ecological succession.

The first plants colonizing a burned forest or abandoned lot aren't just diminished versions of what came before but expressions of nature's remarkable adaptive capacity, with their own particular beauty that exists only because of disruption.

These traditions suggest that finding beauty in breakdown isn't naive optimism but expanded perception—the capacity to see both the real losses and the real emergence that crisis generates simultaneously.

Cultivating this perception might involve:

- Noticing spontaneous community responses to systemic failures
- Appreciating adaptive creativity that emerges specifically through constraint
- Recognizing moments of unexpected connection across previous divides
- Attending to natural processes reclaiming damaged spaces
- Witnessing the particular beauty of impermanence itself

This isn't about minimizing harm or rushing to silver linings. It's about developing perception capacities that can hold both the tragedy of loss and the wonder of emergence simultaneously—a fuller seeing that neither toxic positivity nor doomerism permits.

The Revolutionary Act of Having Fun Anyway

Beyond finding beauty in breakdown lies an even more direct challenge to apocalyptic despair: the deliberate choice to have genuine fun even amid difficult circumstances.

To be clear, this isn't about forced fun, mandatory positivity, or using pleasure to escape reality. It's about the radical insistence that joy remains possible—and necessary—even when systems of power benefit from its absence.

Why might genuine fun qualify as revolutionary in apocalyptic times?

1. Fun directly counters doomism

"Doomism"—the belief that catastrophe is inevitable and resistance futile—serves status quo interests by preemptively defeating challenges to existing arrangements. When enough people believe nothing can change, nothing does change.

Genuine fun—not desperate distraction but authentic enjoyment—embodies the opposite message: that pleasure, connection, and meaning remain possible even in challenging circumstances. It demonstrates experientially what doomism denies theoretically.

2. Fun preserves cultural memory

Systems maintain power partly through historical amnesia—the forgetting of both past oppressions and past resistances. Fun and celebratory practices often preserve cultural memory that official histories erase, maintaining knowledge of what has been and what remains possible.

From traditional songs to community celebrations to intergenerational games, practices of enjoyment carry embedded wisdom about survival, connection, and resilience across time.

3. Fun creates prefigurative spaces

"Prefigurative politics" refers to creating spaces that embody the values you're fighting for rather than just opposing what you're against. Fun and celebration often create prefigurative spaces where different social relations can be temporarily experienced and practiced.

A neighborhood block party, a queer dance night, a community art festival—these aren't just pleasant diversions but laboratories for different ways of being together, making decisions, sharing resources, and valuing contributions.

4. Fun sustains movement relationships

Effective movements require what scholars call "strong ties"—relationships with enough trust and resilience to withstand external pressures and internal conflicts. These ties develop not just through strategic meetings but through shared experiences of enjoyment.

The dance after the protest, the meal after the organizing session, the joke in the middle of a tense moment—these aren't separate from movement building but essential to creating relationships strong enough to sustain collective action over time.

5. Fun interrupts capitalist temporality

Capitalism structures time around productivity, efficiency, and accumulation—making even leisure instrumental rather than intrinsic. Genuine fun interrupts this temporal logic, creating experiences valued for their own sake rather than their productive output.

When you engage in non-productive enjoyment—play without optimization, creativity without monetization, pleasure without purpose—you temporarily step outside capitalist temporal demands, experiencing a different relationship to time itself.

In these ways, having fun during apocalyptic times isn't trivial but transgressive—a direct challenge to systems that require your joylessness to maintain their power.

Practical Approaches to Radical Enjoyment

How might we cultivate radical enjoyment as a resistance practice? Here are some approaches drawn from both historical movements and contemporary communities:

1. Pleasure mapping

Begin by identifying sources of genuine pleasure that remain accessible in your particular circumstances. Not what should be enjoyable or what was enjoyable in the past, but what actually brings joy in your current reality.

This might involve:

- Sensory pleasures (tastes, textures, sounds, scents, visual beauty)
- Relational pleasures (specific interactions with particular people)

- Bodily pleasures (movement, touch, rest, physiological satisfaction)
- Cognitive pleasures (learning, problem-solving, creative thinking)
- Spiritual pleasures (connection to something larger than yourself)

The key is specificity—identifying particular activities, contexts, and experiences that reliably generate genuine enjoyment rather than generic categories.

2. Reclaiming non-productive time

Create deliberate pockets of time dedicated to non-productive enjoyment—activities valued for their intrinsic experience rather than their output or contribution.

This might look like:

- Play without goals or measurement
- Creative expression without audience or evaluation
- Physical movement for sensation rather than fitness
- Learning for curiosity rather than application
- Social connection without networking purpose

Even brief periods of explicitly non-productive enjoyment challenge the capitalist logic that measures all time by its utility.

3. Collective joy practices

While individual pleasures matter, collective joy practices often carry particular political potency by creating shared experiences of connection beyond utilitarian purposes.

Consider:

- Communal meals where the experience is as important as the nutrition
- Dance or movement that synchronizes bodies without competition
- Music that invites participation rather than just consumption
- Games that generate shared enjoyment rather than just winners
- Ceremonies that mark time and transition collectively

These practices build relational resources that can later support more overtly political collective action.

4. Pleasure activism and justice

Explore how your particular struggles for justice intersect with questions of pleasure and joy. Who is denied certain pleasures? Whose joy is criminalized? What pleasures are accessible to whom and on what terms?

As Adrienne Maree Brown suggests, "Pleasure activism is the work we do to reclaim our whole, happy, and satisfiable selves from the impacts, delusions, and limitations of oppression and/or supremacy."

This might involve:

- Supporting decriminalization of consensual activities
- Defending public spaces for non-commercial gathering
- Challenging who is allowed bodily autonomy and expression
- Creating accessibility for diverse experiences of pleasure
- Questioning whose comfort and enjoyment matters in policy

This approach recognizes that the distribution of joy and pleasure in society remains deeply political, with some people's enjoyment protected at others' expense.

5. Celebration as prefiguration

Create celebratory spaces that prefigure the world you're working toward—embodying in temporary form the social relations you hope to make permanent.

This might involve celebrations that:

- Cross conventional social boundaries
- Distribute resources according to need rather than status
- Honor diverse contributions beyond monetary value
- Make decisions through collaborative rather than hierarchical processes
- Create temporary autonomous zones with different operating logics

These prefigurative celebrations offer experiential tastes of alternative possibilities while building collective capacity to manifest them more permanently.

When Enjoyment Feels Impossible

For some reading this chapter, the suggestion that enjoyment could be accessible during apocalyptic times might feel not just challenging but impossible. Trauma, depression, chronic pain, extreme precarity, or acute crisis can genuinely make conventional joy seem unreachable.

˙ If that's your experience, please know:

1. Your difficulty accessing joy isn't personal failure

Systemic factors, traumatic histories, neurological differences, and material conditions genuinely impact capacity for enjoyment. The difficulty isn't a character flaw but a logical response to real circumstances.

2. The smallest moments count

Radical enjoyment doesn't require grand experiences. A single deep breath that feels good, one moment of connection, a brief sensory pleasure—these count. During extremely difficult periods, even microseconds of relief or pleasure matter.

3. Witnessing others' joy has value

When personal enjoyment feels inaccessible, witnessing and supporting others' joy can provide connection to pleasure through relationship rather than direct experience. The capacity to take genuine pleasure in others' enjoyment is itself a form of resistance to isolation.

4. Professional support isn't admitting defeat

Sometimes blocks to enjoyment require professional support to address. Seeking therapy, medication, or other interventions for conditions that prevent pleasure isn't giving up on radical enjoyment but creating conditions where it might become more accessible.

5. Your survival itself is resistance

In the most extreme circumstances, continuing to exist despite systems that benefit from your disappearance is itself a radical act. When active enjoyment feels impossible, simply persisting creates possibility for future pleasure that your absence would preclude.

The political significance of joy doesn't mean everyone must access it equally or constantly. Different people in different circumstances will have vastly different relationships to pleasure during apocalyptic times. The key is recognizing that whatever capacity for enjoyment remains available to you has value—not just personally but politically.

Beyond Mandatory Fun: The Ethics of Enjoyment During Crisis

As we conclude this exploration of radical enjoyment, it's important to address potential concerns about the ethics of pursuing joy amid widespread suffering.

When is enjoyment appropriate?

This question often contains an implicit assumption: that enjoyment during crisis requires special justification, while joylessness is the default ethical response.

But what if we reversed this assumption? What if we recognized that:

- Joy is a natural human capacity, not a special privilege
- Maintaining access to positive emotions supports effective crisis response
- The capacity for enjoyment often correlates with capacity for empathy
- Systems of exploitation benefit from widespread despair

From this perspective, the question shifts from "When is enjoyment justified during crisis?" to "When does crisis response genuinely require temporary suspension of enjoyment?"

This reframing doesn't trivialize suffering or suggest constant celebration regardless of circumstances. It simply recognizes that joy and sorrow, pleasure and pain naturally coexist in human experience—and that maintaining this full emotional range typically supports rather than impairs effective action during difficult times.

Distinguishing types of enjoyment

Not all forms of enjoyment carry the same implications during crisis. We might distinguish between:

Enjoyment that extracts from others

- Requires others' exploitation or exclusion
- Depletes collective resources needed for survival
- Maintains ignorance about harmful systems
- Comes at direct expense of vulnerable people

Enjoyment that builds collective resilience

- Creates or strengthens supportive relationships
- Regenerates resources needed for sustained action
- Maintains awareness of both reality and possibility
- Includes rather than excludes vulnerable perspectives

The ethics lie not in whether enjoyment occurs but in what kind of enjoyment and at whose expense.

The both/and approach

Perhaps most important is rejecting false dichotomies between joy and responsibility, pleasure and awareness, enjoyment and action. Effective crisis response typically requires both/and approaches rather than either/or choices.

We need both:

- Times of focused attention to suffering and times of genuine joy
- Recognition of what's being lost and appreciation of what remains
- Practical action addressing problems and celebration of existing goods
- Solemn acknowledgment of harm and playful creation of alternatives

This both/and orientation isn't moral compromise but ethical complexity—recognition that human beings and human communities function best when able to access their full emotional and experiential range rather than restricting themselves to narrow portions of it.

Conclusion: Joy as Fuel, Not Distraction

Radical enjoyment during apocalyptic times isn't about distracting yourself from reality but fueling your capacity to engage it effectively over the long term. It's not about ignoring suffering but maintaining the emotional, relational, and spiritual resources needed to respond to it without becoming consumed by it.

This approach recognizes that:

- Systems of power often benefit from widespread despair and emotional depletion
- Historical resistance movements have consistently integrated joy and struggle
- Human beings function best with access to their full emotional range
- Prefigurative experiences of the world we desire help make it more achievable

In the next chapter, we'll explore another essential resource for apocalyptic times: humor. Not as escape from difficulty but as a sophisticated cognitive tool for navigating it with both clarity and resilience.

CHAPTER 9: Humor as Survival Skill

"The world is a tragedy to those who feel, but a comedy to those who think." —Horace Walpole

There's a scene I'll never forget from the early pandemic days. I was on a Zoom call with friends, all of us locked down in our respective homes, discussing the latest terrifying news developments. Someone shared a particularly alarming statistic about infection rates, and after a moment of heavy silence, another friend said, "Well, at least the dolphins are returning to the Venice canals," referencing a viral (and later debunked) story about nature "healing" during human isolation.

We all burst into laughter—not because we didn't take the pandemic seriously, but because we did. The laughter wasn't dismissing reality but acknowledging its absurdity. In that moment, humor created a tiny pocket of breathing room in an otherwise suffocating situation.

That's the paradoxical power of humor during apocalyptic times. It doesn't deny the reality of crisis but creates cognitive and emotional space around it—space that allows us to process what might otherwise be too overwhelming to face directly.

In this chapter, we'll explore humor not as escapism but as a sophisticated survival tool—a cognitive, emotional, and social resource that helps human beings navigate even the most challenging circumstances with resilience and clarity.

The Neuroscience of Laughing Through Tears

What exactly happens in our brains and bodies when we laugh, especially during difficult times? The science offers fascinating insights into why humor isn't just pleasant but functional during crisis.

The Stress-Release Mechanism

When we experience a humorous response, our brains process information through multiple parallel pathways:

1. **Cognitive processing:** The prefrontal cortex engages in detecting incongruities, resolving unexpected connections, and processing complex meanings—all classic components of humor.

2. **Emotional activation:** The limbic system, particularly the amygdala and nucleus accumbens, generates the emotional response to humor, including the pleasurable sensations of amusement.

3. **Physical response:** The motor regions trigger laughter—a complex physical response involving facial muscles, vocal apparatus, and often whole-body engagement.

This multi-system activation creates a unique neurological state that directly counteracts stress physiology:

- Laughter reduces cortisol (the primary stress hormone) and increases endorphins (natural pain-killers and mood elevators)
- The physical act of laughing increases oxygen intake and stimulates circulation
- Humor activates the brain's reward pathways, releasing dopamine
- The cognitive processing of humor engages regions associated with perspective-taking and cognitive flexibility

What makes this particularly valuable during crisis is the way humor creates what neuroscientists call a "state shift"—a rapid change in overall nervous system functioning. When we're caught in stress response, our thinking narrows, our perception constricts, and our bodies tense. Humor can interrupt this pattern, creating a brief but significant shift toward a more regulated state.

The Cognitive Mismatch Theory

Research on humor suggests that much of its power comes from detecting and resolving cognitive mismatches—situations where expectations are violated in ways that reveal new perspectives.

During apocalyptic times, we're constantly encountering circumstances that violate our expectations about how the world should work. Humor provides a framework for processing these violations in ways that extract meaning without becoming overwhelmed.

As researcher Rod Martin notes in The Psychology of Humor: "Humor may be viewed as a form of cognitive reappraisal—a way of reinterpreting a threatening situation from a new and less threatening perspective."

This doesn't mean humor makes threats disappear, but it creates cognitive flexibility around them. Instead of being trapped in a single catastrophic interpretation, humor opens alternative perspectives that create room for agency and adaptation.

The Social Synchronization Effect

Perhaps most relevant to crisis resilience is humor's remarkable capacity to synchronize social nervous systems. When people laugh together, research shows:

- Their breathing patterns synchronize
- Their cardiovascular systems show matching activation patterns
- Their neurological stress responses regulate in tandem
- Their attention focuses on shared cognitive frames

This physiological synchronization creates what researcher Stephen Porges calls "co-regulation"—the process by which human nervous systems help stabilize each other during stress.

During apocalyptic times, when individual regulatory capacity is often overtaxed, this social dimension of humor becomes especially valuable. A joke shared during a difficult meeting, a humorous observation during a challenging project, or a funny text during a crisis can create moments of co-regulation that help entire groups maintain functionality under pressure.

These neurological and physiological mechanisms help explain why humor consistently appears as a coping strategy in even the most extreme human circumstances—from concentration camps to natural disasters to medical crises. It's not a frivolous addition to survival but a sophisticated biological mechanism for maintaining cognitive, emotional, and social functioning under extreme stress.

Why Gallows Humor Works (And When It Doesn't)

One particular form of humor often emerges during apocalyptic times: gallows humor—jokes that address dark, threatening, or taboo subjects directly rather than avoiding them. This type of humor has a complex reputation, sometimes seen as inappropriate or insensitive, but research suggests its psychological function is both sophisticated and potentially valuable.

The Psychological Benefits of Gallows Humor

Studies of professionals who regularly encounter crisis and trauma—emergency responders, healthcare workers, disaster relief teams, combat veterans—consistently find gallows humor serving several adaptive functions:

1. Emotional regulation

Dark humor provides indirect ways to acknowledge overwhelming emotions without becoming consumed by them. By transforming terrifying subjects into objects of humor, people create psychological distance that allows processing without overwhelm.

As one emergency physician explained in a research interview: "The jokes aren't about denying the horror. They're about creating just enough space around it to keep functioning when you still have ten more patients to see."

2. Group cohesion

Gallows humor often serves as an in-group signal among people facing similar stressors—a way of communicating "I understand what you're experiencing" without requiring explicit vulnerability.

This creates what sociologists call "communities of coping"—groups united by shared understanding of specific stressors that outsiders may not comprehend. The humor itself becomes a boundary marker identifying who truly understands the situation.

3. Cognitive reframing

Dark humor frequently highlights absurdities and contradictions within terrible situations, creating cognitive frames that make overwhelming realities more psychologically manageable.

By pointing out the ridiculous elements within tragic circumstances, gallows humor asserts that even in horror, meaning-making remains possible—an act of cognitive agency amid conditions that otherwise feel uncontrollable.

4. Status leveling

In hierarchical situations (medical settings, military contexts, disaster zones), gallows humor often serves to temporarily suspend status differences and create more egalitarian communication.

When the senior surgeon and medical student laugh at the same dark joke, a momentary social equality emerges that can facilitate more honest communication about difficult realities.

The Ethics and Limitations of Gallows Humor

Despite these benefits, gallows humor comes with important ethical considerations and limitations:

1. Context and audience matter enormously

Gallows humor typically functions adaptively only among people with shared exposure to the stressor being referenced. The same joke that provides relief for disaster workers might cause harm if shared with disaster survivors or a general audience.

This is because the humor's psychological function depends on shared cognitive frameworks and similar emotional processing needs. Without these shared contexts, dark humor easily becomes insensitive or retraumatizing rather than relieving.

2. Power dynamics affect impact

Gallows humor directed down power gradients (those with more power joking about the suffering of those with less) typically causes harm rather than relief. The same joke might function completely differently depending on who tells it and in what context.

This explains why jokes about oppression made by those experiencing it often serve important psychological and political functions, while the same jokes made by privileged observers typically perpetuate harm.

3. Timing influences reception

What serves as adaptive humor in one phase of crisis may be premature or delayed in another. Research suggests gallows humor typically functions best during active coping phases rather than initial shock or later meaning-making periods.

A joke made too soon may interfere with necessary emotional processing, while the same joke later might facilitate integration of difficult experiences.

4. Individual differences create varied responses

Not everyone processes humor similarly, particularly during stress. Some people find gallows humor essential for coping, while others experience it as distressing or offensive regardless of context.

These differences reflect not just personal preference but variations in psychological processing styles, trauma histories, cultural frameworks, and regulatory needs.

Understanding these nuances helps explain why gallows humor appears so consistently across crisis contexts while simultaneously generating such varied responses. It's neither universally appropriate nor universally inappropriate, but rather a complex psychological tool whose effects depend significantly on context, timing, power dynamics, and individual differences.

The key question becomes not whether dark humor is inherently good or bad during apocalyptic times, but rather: How can we use this psychological mechanism thoughtfully, in ways that support rather than undermine both individual coping and collective care?

Learning to Laugh at the Absurdity of It All

Beyond the specific case of gallows humor lies a broader capacity that supports resilience during apocalyptic times: the ability to recognize and find humor in absurdity itself.

Absurdity arises when expectations and reality diverge dramatically—exactly the conditions that crises create. The systems we relied on malfunction in bizarre ways. Official responses range from inadequate to surreal. Daily life continues alongside extraordinary events, creating jarring juxtapositions.

Learning to laugh at absurdity involves several cognitive shifts:

1. Developing recognition skills

The first step is simply noticing absurdity when it appears. This involves:

- Identifying contradictions between stated goals and actual behaviors
- Noticing surreal juxtapositions in daily experience
- Recognizing patterns of inconsistency in systems and responses
- Attending to the gap between promises and realities

This recognition isn't cynical but clear-sighted—an honest acknowledgment of the often bizarre realities that crises reveal.

2. Cultivating existential perspective

Philosophical traditions dealing with absurdity— from ancient Cynics to modern Existentialists— suggest that humor provides one of the most effective responses to life's fundamental incongruities.

As Albert Camus wrote: "In the midst of winter, I found there was, within me, an invincible summer. And that makes me happy. For it says that no matter how hard the world pushes against me, within me, there's something stronger—something better, pushing right back."

This existential perspective doesn't deny difficulty but creates space to recognize both the genuinely tragic and the genuinely comic aspects of human existence simultaneously.

3. Practicing ironic detachment without cynical disengagement

Ironic humor—the capacity to recognize contradictions without becoming either completely identified with or completely detached from them—provides valuable psychological flexibility during absurd times.

Unlike cynicism, which disengages completely from possibility, irony maintains connection while creating cognitive distance that prevents overwhelming identification. It allows simultaneously acknowledging "this is terrible" and "this is ridiculous"—a both/and perspective that expands response options.

4. Finding community through shared recognition

Perhaps most importantly, humorous responses to absurdity create opportunities for shared recognition—moments of "you see it too?" that combat the isolation that crises often generate.

When someone jokes about the bizarre contradictions in official communications, the surreal experience of continuing mundane activities during extraordinary events, or the strange new social norms emerging from crisis, they create openings for collective acknowledgment of shared reality.

This doesn't solve the underlying problems but prevents the additional suffering that comes from feeling alone in perceiving them.

Humor as Reality Testing

Beyond its emotional benefits, humor serves an important cognitive function during apocalyptic times: reality testing. In environments filled with misinformation, propaganda, and pressure toward either denial or catastrophizing, humor often provides a mechanism for testing perceptions against reality.

Satire as Information Processing

Satirical humor works by exaggerating or highlighting inconsistencies in ways that reveal underlying patterns. During crises, when official narratives often contain significant gaps or contradictions, satire can function as an alternative information processing system.

Consider how political cartoons, comedy news programs, and humorous memes often:

- Identify contradictions in official statements that straight reporting might miss
- Compare rhetoric to actual outcomes in revealing ways
- Highlight patterns of behavior that become obvious only when juxtaposed
- Cut through complexity to identify core dynamics

This isn't just entertainment but a legitimate form of sense-making during periods when conventional information channels may be compromised or overwhelming.

Humor as Propaganda Detection

Research on propaganda resistance shows that humorous processing provides partial protection against manipulative messaging. When people engage information through humorous analysis, they:

- Show increased attention to logical inconsistencies
- Demonstrate greater awareness of emotional manipulation attempts
- Retain more critical distance from authoritative claims
- Process information more actively rather than passively

During apocalyptic times, when crisis often generates both deliberate propaganda and inadvertent misinformation, this protective function becomes particularly valuable.

The Joke as Truth-Teller

Across cultures, humor has historically served as a vehicle for truths that might be dangerous to state directly. From medieval court jesters to contemporary political comedians, the partially protected status of "just joking" creates space for observations that might otherwise be suppressed.

As communication theorist Peter McGraw notes: "The psychological distance created by humor allows people to engage with ideas that might otherwise be threatening or overwhelming."

During apocalyptic times, when direct confrontation with certain realities might trigger either external censorship or internal resistance, humor can create backdoor access to truths we need but struggle to face directly.

The Limits of Humorous Reality Testing

While humor provides valuable reality-testing functions, it also has significant limitations:

- Humor can oversimplify complex situations for comic effect
- The emotional relief of humor might sometimes substitute for necessary action
- Not all audiences process humorous information with equal critical awareness
- Humor itself can be weaponized as propaganda or misdirection

These limitations don't negate humor's value for reality testing but suggest it functions best as one component of a diverse sense-making toolkit rather than a standalone strategy.

Developing Your Apocalyptic Humor Style

Just as people have different emotional processing needs and cognitive styles, they also have different relationships to humor during difficult times. Developing your personal approach to apocalyptic humor involves both self-awareness and skill development.

Understanding Your Humor Processing Style

Research identifies several distinct approaches to processing difficulty through humor:

1. **Affiliative humor:** Finding comedy that connects you with others through shared recognition of absurdity
2. **Self-enhancing humor:** Using humor to maintain perspective on your own challenges and limitations
3. **Aggressive humor:** Targeting frustration at deserving systems or power structures (rather than vulnerable individuals)
4. **Self-deprecating humor:** Finding comedy in your own responses to crisis without undermining genuine needs

Most people naturally gravitate toward certain styles, but all can be developed with practice. The key is identifying which approaches:

- Feel authentic rather than forced
- Create genuine relief rather than additional tension
- Connect rather than isolate you from important others
- Support cognitive flexibility rather than rigidity

Humor Boundaries and Ethics

Especially during apocalyptic times, developing clear boundaries around humor becomes important. Some considerations include:

1. **Direction of humor**
- Humor targeting powerful systems versus vulnerable individuals
- Joking about your own experience versus others' suffering
- Satire directed at responses to problems versus the affected people
2. **Context awareness**
- Who comprises your audience and what's their relationship to the subject?
- What power dynamics exist in the humor situation?

- Is the timing appropriate given processing needs?
3. **Intent and impact alignment**
- Does your humor's impact match your intentions?
- Are you open to feedback about unintended effects?
- Do you prioritize connection over being clever?

These boundaries aren't about policing humor but ensuring it serves its adaptive functions rather than creating additional harm during already difficult circumstances.

Building Your Humor Toolkit

Like any coping skill, humor can be intentionally developed. Some approaches include:

1. **Curating external humor resources**
- Identify comedians whose perspective helps you process difficulty
- Collect memes, videos, or articles that reliably shift your perspective
- Create a humor emergency kit for especially challenging moments
2. **Practicing humorous reframing**
- When facing a difficult situation, challenge yourself to find one genuinely funny aspect

- Look for the absurd elements within serious circumstances
- Notice unexpected juxtapositions in daily apocalyptic living

3. **Finding humor buddies**
- Identify people with compatible humor styles for processing challenges
- Create contexts where humorous perspectives are explicitly welcome
- Develop inside jokes that efficiently reference shared absurd experiences

4. **Using humor journaling**
- Record bizarre or incongruous moments as they occur
- Write dialogues exploring the humorous aspects of challenging situations
- Create satirical versions of official communications or news

These practices don't aim to transform genuinely tragic situations into comedy but to develop the cognitive flexibility that humor provides as a resource for navigating difficult circumstances.

When Humor Isn't Helping

While humor offers valuable psychological, social, and cognitive benefits during apocalyptic times, it's not universally helpful in all situations. Recognizing when humor isn't serving adaptive functions becomes an important discernment skill.

Signs That Humor May Be Functioning Maladaptively

1. **When humor consistently prevents necessary emotional processing**
- Using jokes to immediately shut down any serious discussion
- Feeling unable to engage sincerely with important topics
- Finding that humor creates emotional numbness rather than flexibility
2. **When humor reinforces harmful patterns**
- Jokes that punch down rather than up
- Humor that consistently undermines your own legitimate needs
- Comic perspectives that increase rather than decrease prejudice
3. **When humor creates rather than bridges isolation**
- Finding yourself humorously disconnected from all perspectives
- Using inside jokes to exclude rather than include
- Noticing increased alienation after humorous exchanges

4. **When humor substitutes for necessary action**
- Joking about problems exclusively rather than addressing them
- Using comedy to distance from responsibility
- Finding humor decreases rather than increases engagement

In these situations, humor may need modulation, contextual adjustment, or temporary suspension to allow other adaptive processes to occur.

Alternative Approaches When Humor Isn't Appropriate

When circumstances make humor either unhelpful or inappropriate, several alternative approaches can provide similar psychological benefits:

1. **Direct acknowledgment** Sometimes simply naming the difficulty directly creates the same psychological space that humor attempts to generate indirectly. "This is genuinely overwhelming right now" can provide similar relief to a joke in certain contexts.

2. **Meaning-focused engagement** When humor feels inappropriate, connecting to deeper purpose and values can provide

alternative psychological resources. Asking "What matters most right now?" can create perspective without requiring comic distance.

3. **Present-moment grounding** In situations where humor might function as avoidance, direct sensory engagement with the present moment can provide regulatory benefits without either denial or overwhelm. Simple practices like noticing five things you can see, four you can touch, etc., create similar state shifts to humor.

4. **Structured emotional processing** When the situation requires direct emotional engagement that humor might short-circuit, structured approaches like writing exercises, established rituals, or facilitated discussions can provide containment without avoidance.

These alternatives don't replace humor but complement it—expanding the toolkit for navigating difficult circumstances adaptively.

Humor as Resistance

Beyond its psychological functions, humor has historically served as an effective resistance strategy during oppressive conditions—a role particularly relevant during apocalyptic times when various forms of authoritarianism often emerge or intensify.

Historical Examples of Resistance Humor

From Nazi-occupied Europe to Soviet Russia to authoritarian regimes worldwide, humor has consistently emerged as both psychological support and political strategy:

1. **World War II resistance jokes** Under Nazi occupation, jokes spread through underground networks, maintaining morale and undermining occupier legitimacy. As one Dutch resistance member later recalled: "Every joke we told was a tiny act of rebellion. They could control our actions but not our minds."

2. **Soviet political humor** Throughout the Soviet era, political jokes served as vehicles for truths that couldn't be stated directly. As historian Ben Lewis documents in "Hammer and Tickle," this humor created alternative information networks that maintained critical thinking despite official propaganda.

3. **Contemporary authoritarianism responses** From Chinese internet memes evading censorship through coded language to Middle Eastern satire during the Arab Spring, humor continues to function as a resistance tool in repressive contexts worldwide.

These historical examples suggest humor's potential as more than just psychological relief but actual political resistance during apocalyptic periods.

How Humor Functions as Resistance

Research on humor under authoritarian conditions identifies several specific resistance functions:

1. **Legitimacy undermining** Humor targets the gap between official claims and lived reality,

eroding regime legitimacy. By highlighting absurdities, contradictions, and hypocrisies, jokes make it harder to maintain the illusion of authority's reasonableness or inevitability.

2. **Solidarity building** Shared jokes create invisible communities of resistance—people who recognize the same contradictions and refuse the same narratives. This builds psychological solidarity that can later support more direct collective action.

3. **Censorship evasion** Humor's ambiguity and deniability ("I was just joking!") allows communication that might otherwise be blocked. The cognitive indirection of humor creates channels for information exchange when direct communication becomes dangerous.

4. **Morale maintenance** Perhaps most fundamentally, humor preserves psychological resources necessary for long-term resistance. By preventing complete identification with oppressive narratives, humor maintains the cognitive and emotional

capacity to imagine alternatives.

Contemporary Applications

In current apocalyptic contexts, these resistance functions remain relevant across various situations:

1. **Corporate narrative resistance** Workplace humor often targets the gap between company values statements and actual practices. These jokes aren't just venting but active resistance to corporate reality distortion fields.

2. **Crisis management critique** During disasters, humor frequently highlights the absurdities of official response—not just for psychological relief but to maintain critical perspective on management failures.

3. **Propaganda immunity** When media environments become saturated with manipulation attempts, humor provides partial immunity by maintaining critical distance from official narratives regardless of source.

4. **Surveillance resistance** In increasingly surveilled environments, humor's ambiguity and plausible deniability create communication spaces partially protected from algorithmic and human monitoring.

These applications don't suggest humor alone creates political change but recognize its role in maintaining the psychological conditions where more direct action remains possible.

Conclusion: The Serious Work of Humor

As we conclude this exploration of humor as a survival skill, it's worth emphasizing that taking humor seriously doesn't mean treating everything as a joke. Quite the opposite—it means recognizing humor's legitimate functions in maintaining the cognitive, emotional, and social resources required for long-term navigation of genuinely difficult circumstances.

The research and historical evidence consistently show that humor during apocalyptic times isn't a frivolous addition to "serious" coping strategies but an integral component of resilient response. Its cognitive, emotional, physiological, and social benefits provide resources that no amount of solemn analysis alone can generate.

This doesn't mean forcing humor when it doesn't arise naturally or using it to avoid necessary engagement with difficult realities. It means allowing humor its proper place in the complex ecosystem of human responses to crisis—neither elevating it as a magical solution nor dismissing it as inappropriate levity.

In the midst of flames, a well-timed joke doesn't extinguish the fire but might just create the moment of clarity, connection, or courage needed to find the next step forward. And sometimes, that brief moment makes all the difference between being consumed by the apocalypse and finding a way through it—perhaps even laughing as you go.

PART IV: PRACTICAL APOCALYPSE SKILLS

CHAPTER 10: Micro-Thriving

If you've ever felt guilty for celebrating a small victory while the world burns, this chapter is for you.

If you've ever wondered whether it even matters to accomplish anything when everything feels broken, this chapter is for you.

If you've ever been told that your focus on getting through the day is "too small" or "not ambitious enough," this chapter is especially for you.

In apocalyptic times, conventional notions of success and achievement often become simultaneously unattainable and irrelevant. The career ladder might be on fire. The five-year plan might be laughable. The standard metrics of progress might no longer apply to a world in flux.

Yet humans need a sense of efficacy and accomplishment to maintain psychological wellbeing. We're wired to derive meaning from making progress, however that's defined. When all forms of forward movement seem blocked, many people experience a profound sense of stagnation that can spiral into helplessness and despair.

This is where micro-thriving becomes essential. Not as a diminished substitute for "real" achievement, but as a legitimate approach to creating meaningful forward movement within the actual conditions of your life.

The Art of the Five-Minute Win

At the core of micro-thriving is the five-minute win —a small, achievable action that creates a genuine sense of completion and progress, regardless of external circumstances.

These aren't imaginary victories or participation trophies. They're real accomplishments, just at a scale that remains possible even when larger achievements feel out of reach.

Some examples of five-minute wins:

- Clearing one small space in a chaotic environment
- Sending that text you've been avoiding
- Completing a single focused work task
- Making a decision you've been postponing
- Taking the first step on a project that feels overwhelming
- Successfully navigating a challenging interaction
- Learning one useful piece of information
- Finding a solution to a minor but irritating problem

What makes these "wins" rather than just tasks is that they generate a genuine sense of efficacy— the feeling that you can take action that matters, even in small ways.

This feeling is neurologically significant. When we experience even small victories, our brains release dopamine, which not only creates momentary pleasure but strengthens the neural pathways associated with that behavior. This makes future action more likely and builds momentum from tiny successes toward larger capacities.

The five-minute win approach isn't about lowering standards. It's about creating attainable standards that generate the neurochemical and psychological resources needed for continued effort. Rather than waiting for major achievements to feel effective (which may not come in apocalyptic conditions), this approach deliberately creates micro-experiences of efficacy that sustain motivation through difficult periods.

Designing Effective Five-Minute Wins

Not all small tasks qualify as effective five-minute wins. The most psychologically supportive micro-achievements typically share certain characteristics:

1. **Clear completion point** The most effective micro-wins have an unambiguous ending—a specific moment when you can say "it's done" rather than "it's better" or "it's progressing." This completion trigger provides the dopamine-releasing satisfaction that builds momentum.

2. **Authentic value** Effective micro-wins genuinely matter to you—they solve a real problem, create actual value, or address something you authentically care about. Artificial tasks created solely for the sake of completion rarely generate the same psychological benefits.

3. **Appropriate challenge level** The most motivating micro-wins require some effort but remain definitely achievable. Too easy, and they feel meaningless; too difficult, and they become discouraging. The sweet spot is tasks that stretch your current capacity just slightly.

4. **Tangible results** Wins with visible, sensory, or otherwise perceivable outcomes tend to generate stronger efficacy experiences than completely abstract achievements. Being able to see, touch, hear, or otherwise experience the result strengthens the completion sense.

5. **Personal agency** Effective micro-wins involve factors within your control rather than dependent on external approval or circumstances. This creates a direct experience of cause and effect—your action leads directly to the outcome.

Using these characteristics, you can design personalized five-minute wins tailored to your specific circumstances, values, and challenges. The goal isn't completing arbitrary tasks but deliberately creating experiences of agency and accomplishment that generate resources for continued functioning.

Five-Minute Win Categories

To help identify potential micro-wins in your own life, consider these common categories:

1. Environment wins

- Clearing one surface in a cluttered space
- Fixing one broken item
- Improving one sensory aspect of your surroundings (light, sound, smell)
- Organizing one small category of possessions

- Removing one piece of digital clutter

2. Body wins

- Completing one brief physical movement sequence
- Preparing one nourishing food item
- Taking one concrete step to improve comfort
- Addressing one minor health concern
- Giving attention to one neglected bodily need

3. Relationship wins

- Having one difficult conversation you've been avoiding
- Setting one boundary clearly
- Expressing one genuine appreciation
- Asking for one specific form of help
- Making one meaningful connection

4. Work/Contribution wins

- Completing one discrete work task
- Making one decision that unblocks progress
- Helping one person with a specific need
- Teaching one skill or piece of information
- Creating one small useful or beautiful thing

5. Knowledge wins

- Learning one practical skill
- Understanding one complex concept
- Finding one piece of needed information
- Clarifying one confusing situation
- Making one connection between previously separate ideas

6. System wins

- Creating one small process improvement
- Automating one repetitive task
- Eliminating one unnecessary step
- Adding one helpful prompt or reminder
- Removing one friction point from a regular activity

The specific content of your five-minute wins will depend on your circumstances, values, and current challenges. The key is identifying actions that genuinely generate that sense of "I accomplished something meaningful, however small" rather than just checking boxes.

Celebrating Survival-Level Accomplishments

Beyond intentional five-minute wins lies another crucial aspect of micro-thriving: recognizing when survival itself represents genuine achievement. In particularly difficult circumstances, actions that might seem basic in normal times can require significant effort and therefore deserve acknowledgment as legitimate accomplishments.

This isn't about lowering standards but about calibrating them to actual conditions. Just as an Olympic feat in thin mountain air would be evaluated differently than the same performance at sea level, achievements during crisis need contextual evaluation rather than comparison to non-crisis expectations.

Some examples of survival-level accomplishments that deserve recognition:

- **Basic self-care during depression** - When mental health challenges make even fundamental self-maintenance difficult, completing actions like showering, eating regularly, or maintaining minimal order represent genuine achievements.

- **Continued functioning during acute grief** - In periods of significant loss, simply continuing to fulfill basic responsibilities can require tremendous effort worthy of acknowledgment.

- **Maintaining boundaries during crisis** - When systems are breaking down, preserving necessary personal boundaries often requires creativity and courage that merits recognition.

- **Navigating new constraints** - Adapting to sudden limitations—whether physical, financial, social, or environmental—involves significant learning and adjustment that constitutes real achievement.

- **Emotional regulation during trauma** - Managing emotional responses while processing traumatic experiences represents sophisticated psychological work deserving respect.

These accomplishments might not appear on conventional achievement lists, but they involve real effort, skill development, and personal resources. Recognizing them as legitimate achievements isn't "settling" but accurately acknowledging the genuine work involved in navigating difficult circumstances.

The Challenge of Recalibration

For many people, recognizing survival-level accomplishments requires significant cognitive recalibration. Those who previously measured themselves by conventional achievement metrics often struggle to value these more fundamental forms of success.

Some approaches that help with this recalibration:

1. **Effort-based rather than outcome-based evaluation** Instead of judging solely by results, consider the effort required given your current circumstances. The same outcome might represent vastly different achievement levels depending on what obstacles were overcome to reach it.

2. **Contextual rather than absolute standards** Rather than comparing to abstract ideals or pre-crisis capabilities, evaluate based on what's possible within current constraints. This isn't lowering standards but making them relevant to actual conditions.

3. **Expert recognition** Professionals who work regularly with crisis and trauma—therapists, disaster responders, grief counselors—consistently affirm the genuine achievement represented by survival-level functioning during difficult periods. Their expert perspective can help legitimate this recalibration.

4. **Historical examples** Throughout history, individuals navigating extreme circumstances—from war zones to refugee experiences to natural disasters—have recognized the legitimate accomplishment of maintaining basic functioning and dignity amid crisis. This historical context helps validate similar recognition in current circumstances.

5. **Resource-aware assessment** Consider what personal, social, material, and systemic resources were available for any given task. When resources are limited, accomplishments that might seem basic in resource-rich environments represent significant achievements.

This recalibration isn't about permanent lowering of aspirations but about accurate assessment of what constitutes achievement in specific contexts. Just as we wouldn't expect identical athletic performance in all environmental conditions, we shouldn't expect identical achievement definitions across vastly different life circumstances.

Why "Just Getting Through" Is Sometimes Heroic

Beyond recognizing survival-level accomplishments lies an even more fundamental aspect of micro-thriving: acknowledging when simply continuing represents a heroic act.

In certain circumstances, the choice to keep going —to face another day, to stay present, to remain engaged with difficult realities—reflects profound courage that deserves recognition not as failure to thrive but as a legitimate form of thriving given the circumstances.

The Heroism of Continuation

Why might "just getting through" sometimes constitute heroic action? Consider:

1. **Resistance to dehumanization** In contexts that devalue human dignity, simply maintaining your humanity—your capacity for connection, care, and meaning—represents resistance to forces that would reduce you to mere survival.

As Holocaust survivor and psychiatrist Viktor Frankl observed of concentration camp experiences: "The last of human freedoms—to choose one's attitude in any given set of circumstances, to choose one's own way." This freedom to choose how one faces overwhelming circumstances represents a profound form of human accomplishment.

2. **Testimony through presence** In situations where powerful forces benefit from your erasure or silence, continuing to exist and bear witness constitutes significant action. Your continued presence ensures experiences aren't forgotten or denied.

As author Rebecca Solnit notes: "To survive trauma, one must be able to tell the story of it." Sometimes, being present enough to eventually tell the story requires all available resources and represents a genuine achievement.

3. **Preservation of possibility** Continuing through periods where positive outcomes

seem impossible preserves the possibility of future change that current abandonment would foreclose. This preservation of possibility, when no immediate path forward is visible, can require tremendous courage and vision.

As civil rights leader Bayard Rustin observed: "We need in every community a group of angelic troublemakers...people who have a deep dissatisfaction with things as they are and who want to change them." Sometimes being that "troublemaker" simply means refusing to accept current conditions as final, even when alternatives aren't yet visible.

4. **Relational responsibility** For those with dependents or significant relationships, continuing to show up despite personal difficulty often reflects a profound commitment to others that transcends individual achievement metrics.

When your continuation supports others' wellbeing —whether children, family members, community responsibilities, or even companion animals—"just getting through" becomes not mere survival but active care work.

In these contexts, reframing continuation from "mere survival" to "heroic persistence" isn't romanticizing difficulty but accurately recognizing the genuine accomplishment represented by choosing to remain engaged with life despite overwhelming circumstances.

Recognition Practices for Continuation

How might we effectively recognize this form of heroism without glorifying suffering? Some approaches include:

1. **Marking continued presence** Simple rituals that acknowledge ongoing engagement with life—lighting candles on difficult anniversaries, noting personal or collective endurance milestones, creating tangible representations of persistence—provide concrete recognition of this form of accomplishment.

2. **Collecting continuation evidence** Keeping tangible records of having continued—journals, photographs, artifacts, or other documentation of "still here" moments—creates visible evidence of this often invisible form of achievement.

3. **Celebrating the choice to continue**
Explicitly acknowledging the decision to keep going as an active choice rather than passive default recognizes the agency involved in continuation. "You chose to face today" honors the deliberate nature of this achievement.

4. **Witnessing others' persistence** Actively acknowledging others who continue despite difficulty—not with empty platitudes like "you're so strong" but with specific recognition of the courage their continuation represents—creates cultures where this form of accomplishment receives appropriate recognition.

5. **Legacy awareness** Connecting current continuation to historical examples of persistence that later enabled significant change helps contextualize this form of achievement within larger narratives of human resilience and transformation.

These practices don't glorify suffering or suggest that mere continuation is the ultimate goal. Rather, they accurately recognize the genuine accomplishment represented by choosing engagement over disengagement when the former requires significantly more resources than the latter.

Creating Momentum Through Micro-Achievements

While recognizing survival-level accomplishments provides essential validation during difficult periods, most people eventually seek to move beyond mere continuation toward more active forms of thriving. The challenge becomes: How do you build momentum when conventional achievement paths are disrupted?

This is where strategic micro-achievements become particularly valuable—not just as standalone wins but as deliberate stepping stones toward larger capacities.

The Momentum Principle

Research on motivation and achievement consistently shows that progress begets progress. Even small forward movements create psychological and neurological resources that facilitate larger subsequent actions.

This "momentum principle" operates through several mechanisms:

1. **Self-efficacy reinforcement** Each successful action, however small, strengthens belief in your capacity to affect outcomes. This increased self-efficacy makes attempting larger actions more likely.

2. **Positive emotion generation** Achievements generate positive emotions that broaden perception and build resources. These expanded psychological assets support more ambitious subsequent efforts.

3. **Implementation knowledge** Small successes provide practical information about what works, creating transferable knowledge that improves efficiency of future actions.

4. **Identity reinforcement** Micro-achievements gradually shift self-concept from "someone who can't" to "someone who can," making

larger achievements feel more congruent with identity.

Understanding these mechanisms allows for strategic sequencing of micro-achievements to build maximum momentum toward larger capacities.

Momentum-Building Sequences

Rather than viewing micro-achievements as random acts, consider designing deliberate sequences that progressively build capacity in specific domains:

Example: Writing Capacity Sequence

1. Write one sentence
2. Write for five minutes
3. Complete one paragraph
4. Write daily for one week
5. Complete one short piece
6. Share writing with one trusted person
7. Submit to one low-stakes opportunity
8. Develop one writing project

Example: Social Reconnection Sequence

1. Send one text message
2. Have one brief conversation
3. Arrange one low-demand meetup
4. Participate in one group activity
5. Initiate one meaningful exchange
6. Maintain one regular connection
7. Navigate one difficult interaction
8. Build one supportive friendship

Example: Work Capacity Sequence

1. Complete one simple task
2. Work focused for 15 minutes
3. Finish one challenging component
4. Achieve one meaningful deliverable
5. Develop one improved process
6. Take on one significant responsibility
7. Lead one collaborative effort
8. Complete one major project

These sequences aren't rigid prescriptions but illustrations of how deliberately structured micro-achievements can build progressive capacity rather than remaining isolated wins.

The key principles for effective momentum sequences include:

1. **Gradual progression** Each step should be achievable from the previous position while

representing genuine forward movement.

2. **Success likelihood** Early sequence steps should have very high success probability (80%+) to establish momentum, with challenge increasing gradually as capacity develops.

3. **Skill transferability** Each achievement should develop capacities applicable to subsequent steps rather than isolated abilities.

4. **Meaningful milestones** The sequence should include regular "completion points" that provide satisfaction rather than endless incremental steps.

5. **Flexibility with direction** While maintaining progressive challenge, the sequence should remain adaptable to changing conditions and emerging opportunities.

By deliberately structuring micro-achievements into these kind of progressive sequences, you can transform isolated wins into sustained capacity development even in challenging circumstances.

The Five-Minute Focus Method

One specific micro-thriving technique deserves special attention: the five-minute focus method. This approach provides a structured way to generate micro-achievements when attention, motivation, or energy are severely limited.

The Basic Protocol

The five-minute focus method consists of:

1. **Select one specific, completable task** Choose something small enough to finish in a brief focused period, with a clear endpoint.

2. **Set a literal timer for five minutes** The physical act of setting a timer creates a concrete container for the effort.

3. **Work with complete focus for exactly five minutes** During this period, give undivided attention to the task without diversion.

4. **Stop when the timer sounds** Whether the task is complete or not, honor the time boundary.

5. **Acknowledge the effort regardless of outcome** Recognize the achievement of focused attention, separate from task completion.

6. **Decide whether to continue for another five minutes** After a brief pause, determine whether to continue or switch activities.

This method provides several benefits particularly valuable during apocalyptic times:

- **Extremely low initial commitment barrier** Anyone can commit to just five minutes, making it accessible even during severe motivation or energy deficits.

- **Protection against both under-effort and over-effort** The structure prevents both avoidance and the exhaustion that comes from pushing beyond sustainable limits.

- **Attention training** Regular practice develops focused attention capacity, a resource often depleted during crisis.

- **Experience separation from outcome** The focus on effort rather than completion helps develop non-attachment to results while still taking action.

- **Progressive capacity building** Over time, both focus duration and task complexity can increase gradually as capacity develops.

Variations for Different Circumstances

The basic protocol can be adapted for specific conditions:

For severe executive function challenges:

- Reduce to one-minute intervals
- Include physical movement between intervals
- Use external body-based cues (like breath counting)
- Incorporate sensory anchors (specific sounds, objects, etc.)

For anxiety-related focusing difficulties:

- Begin with 30 seconds of deliberate nervous system regulation
- Choose tasks with sensory engagement components
- Include explicit permission to stop if overwhelm occurs
- Pair with physiological support (grounding objects, etc.)

For energy conservation needs:

- Build in mandatory rest periods between intervals
- Scale physical demands based on energy assessment
- Include energy tracking before/after for calibration
- Prioritize high-value tasks for limited energy expenditure

For intrusive thought patterns:

- Add brief thought acknowledgment practice between intervals
- Incorporate simple thought anchors during focus periods
- Reduce environmental triggers during sessions
- Include compassionate redirection for thought wandering

For isolation-related motivation challenges:

- Create virtual accountability partnerships
- Share five-minute intentions with others
- Report completions to supportive connections
- Develop parallel working sessions even on different tasks

These variations maintain the core structure while addressing specific barriers that might otherwise prevent even micro-achievement experiences.

Building Identity Through Micro-Narratives

Beyond discrete achievements, micro-thriving also involves constructing narratives that connect these small wins into meaningful identity development. Even when conventional achievement narratives are disrupted, micro-narratives provide continuity of self through difficult transitions.

The Power of Micro-Narratives

Micro-narratives are simply small stories we tell about our experiences and actions—brief accounts that create meaning from otherwise disconnected events. During apocalyptic times, these small stories become particularly important for maintaining coherent identity when larger life narratives are disrupted.

Research on narrative identity shows that people who can construct meaning from their experiences —even difficult ones—demonstrate greater resilience than those who experience events as random or meaningless. Micro-narratives provide accessible meaning-making even when comprehensive understanding isn't possible.

Some effective forms of micro-narratives include:

1. **Adaptation stories** Narratives focused on how you've adjusted to changing circumstances, highlighting flexibility and learning rather than achievement of predetermined goals.

Example: "I figured out three new ways to connect with people when in-person gathering became impossible."

2. **Contribution narratives** Stories about how your actions, however small, benefited others or systems beyond yourself, creating meaning through impact rather than scale.

Example: "I helped one person understand how to access resources they needed during a confusing time."

3. **Continuity threads** Narratives that identify consistent values or qualities expressed across different circumstances, providing identity stability amid external change.

Example: "Even when everything else changed, I maintained my commitment to creating moments of beauty."

4. **Capacity development arcs** Stories tracking the development of new skills or strengths specifically in response to challenging conditions.

Example: "I've become someone who can navigate uncertainty with more grace than I could before."

5. **Connection preservation tales** Narratives about maintaining important relationships despite disruption, centering relational rather than individual achievement.

Example: "We found ways to support each other even when conventional gatherings became impossible."

These micro-narratives don't deny difficulty or pretend small actions equal large ones. Rather, they create authentic meaning from actual experiences, preserving identity coherence when conventional achievement narratives no longer apply.

Practices for Developing Micro-Narratives

Several practical approaches support the development of these identity-preserving micro-narratives:

1. **Regular reflection moments** Brief, structured reflection periods—even just 5 minutes daily or weekly—focused on identifying meaningful moments or actions.

Prompt examples:

- "One small thing I did that mattered was..."
- "Something I learned about myself recently is..."
- "A moment when I expressed my values was..."

2. **Physical documentation** Tangible records of micro-achievements and their meaning—journals, voice memos, photographs, collected objects—that make these moments concrete rather than ephemeral.

3. **Sharing structures** Regular opportunities to share micro-narratives with supportive others, whether through direct conversation, digital exchanges, or group reflection practices.

4. **Progressive integration** Periodically reviewing collected micro-narratives to identify emerging patterns and gradually construct larger meaning frameworks.

5. **Alternative measurement markers** Developing personalized metrics for "progress" or "achievement" that match current realities rather than applying mismatched conventional measures.

These practices don't require extensive time or resources but provide crucial support for identity coherence during periods when conventional achievement narratives no longer fit lived experience.

When Micro-Thriving Isn't Enough

While micro-thriving provides essential support during apocalyptic times, integrity requires acknowledging its limitations. There are circumstances where focusing exclusively on micro-achievements may be insufficient or even counterproductive.

Recognizing Systemic Barriers to Thriving

Sometimes the primary obstacles to thriving aren't individual capacity limitations but systemic barriers that require collective rather than personal response. In these cases, exclusive focus on micro-thriving might inadvertently reinforce harmful systems by individualizing structural problems.

Signs that systemic factors may be primary:

- Similar patterns affect many people regardless of individual efforts
- Private achievements consistently face public undermining
- Resources necessary for thriving are systematically withheld
- Individual "success stories" require exceptional privilege or luck
- Collective action consistently produces better outcomes than individual effort

In these situations, effective thriving may require balancing micro-achievement with appropriate system engagement—not because personal achievements don't matter, but because their sustainability requires addressing larger contexts.

Balancing Micro and Macro Approaches

Rather than seeing micro-thriving and system change as opposed, consider how they might complement each other:

1. **Sustainable activation** Micro-achievements can build the personal resources necessary for effective system engagement, preventing burnout while maintaining capacity for larger action.

2. **Prefigurative practice** Small-scale successes can demonstrate alternative possibilities that inform larger change efforts, providing concrete examples rather than just abstract visions.

3. **Resilience during slow change** Micro-thriving can sustain wellbeing during the often lengthy periods required for system transformation, preventing despair during inevitable delays and setbacks.

4. **Bridging immediate and ultimate needs** The micro-achievement approach helps balance addressing urgent present needs while working toward longer-term structural improvements.

5. **Skill development for larger change** Many capacities developed through micro-thriving—focused attention, progress perception, momentum building—transfer directly to more systemic change work.

This balanced approach neither dismisses the importance of personal thriving nor ignores the reality that individual flourishing ultimately requires supportive systems.

When to Seek Additional Support

Beyond systemic considerations, certain personal circumstances may require support beyond micro-thriving strategies. Signs that additional assistance might be beneficial include:

- Persistent inability to experience accomplishment from any actions
- Increasing rather than decreasing difficulty with basic functioning
- Thoughts of harm to self or others
- Complete inability to envision any positive future
- Significant dissociation or reality detachment

These experiences don't represent failure at micro-thriving but indicate that current challenges exceed what self-directed strategies alone can address. Seeking appropriate professional support in these circumstances represents self-care rather than defeat.

Resources for various forms of additional support are included in the appendix, with options ranging from crisis intervention to longer-term assistance across different accessibility levels.

Conclusion: The Revolutionary Nature of Micro-Thriving

As we conclude this exploration of micro-thriving, it's worth emphasizing that these approaches aren't merely coping mechanisms for diminished circumstances but potentially revolutionary practices in a culture obsessed with grand achievement and constant productivity.

By recalibrating our understanding of what constitutes meaningful achievement, micro-thriving doesn't just help us navigate apocalyptic times—it challenges fundamental assumptions about human value, success, and purpose that deserve questioning regardless of external conditions.

The micro-thriving perspective suggests that:

1. **Human worth isn't measured by productivity or achievement** Recognizing the legitimacy of survival-level

accomplishments affirms inherent human value separate from conventional success metrics.

2. **Meaningful action exists at every scale** Finding value in five-minute wins challenges the bias toward grand gestures and outcomes, revealing significance in everyday actions often dismissed as trivial.

3. **Context matters in evaluating accomplishment** Acknowledging how circumstances affect achievement possibilities challenges the myth of pure meritocracy and universal standards.

4. **Progress isn't always linear or visible** Valuing maintenance and continuation during difficult periods recognizes forms of achievement that conventional progress narratives render invisible.

5. **Connection often matters more than accomplishment** Prioritizing relational responsibility over individual achievement

challenges deeply individualistic success concepts.

These perspectives offer not just survival strategies for apocalyptic times but potential foundations for more humane and sustainable approaches to human thriving beyond current crises.

The five-minute win might seem like a small concession to difficult circumstances. But perhaps it's also an invitation to reconsider what truly constitutes a life well-lived—a question worth exploring regardless of whether the world is literally or metaphorically burning around us.

In the next chapter, we'll explore another essential apocalyptic skill: managing the overwhelming flood of information, emotion, and demands that often accompanies crisis periods.

CHAPTER 11: Managing Apocalypse Overwhelm

There's a particular feeling unique to apocalyptic times—a sensation of being simultaneously frozen and frantic, paralyzed by too many threats yet frantically trying to respond to all of them. Your attention fragments into a thousand pieces. Your emotions spike and crash in unpredictable waves. Your capacity feels ridiculously insufficient compared to the magnitude of challenges.

I call this state "apocalypse overwhelm." It's not ordinary stress or garden-variety anxiety. It's a specific response to circumstances where:

- Multiple serious threats exist simultaneously

- Information about these threats constantly changes
- Clear action paths are either absent or contradictory
- Both action and inaction potentially carry significant consequences
- The systems you relied on for stability are themselves destabilizing

This chapter isn't about eliminating these conditions—that would require systemic change beyond individual control. Instead, we'll explore practical approaches for maintaining functionality when apocalypse overwhelm is a reasonable response to actual circumstances rather than a personal failing.

Practical Tools for Days When Everything Is Too Much

Before diving into broader strategies, let's begin with immediate tools for acute overwhelm moments —those days when you wake up already drowning in too much input, too many demands, and too few resources to meet them.

1. The Emergency Reset Protocol

When overwhelm reaches the point where even deciding what to do next becomes impossible, this structured reset provides a pathway back to minimal functionality:

Step 1: Physiological stabilization (5 minutes)

- Place one hand on your chest and one on your abdomen
- Take 5-10 deliberately slow breaths, extending exhales
- Drink a full glass of water
- If possible, step outside or look out a window for 30 seconds
- Engage in 60 seconds of physical movement (anything from stretching to jumping jacks)

Step 2: Environmental simplification (5 minutes)

- Silence all non-emergency notifications
- Clear the surface directly in front of you
- Reduce sensory input (adjust light, noise, temperature if possible)
- Close unnecessary digital windows/apps
- Put away any non-essential items in your immediate space

Step 3: Attention convergence (5 minutes)

- On one sheet of paper or one digital note:
- Write down every task/concern currently occupying mental space
- Circle the 1-3 items that are genuinely time-sensitive today
- Highlight the 1 item requiring attention in the next hour
- Draw a box around concerns that can't be addressed through immediate action

Step 4: Single-action initiation (5 minutes)

- Select one small, completable action related to your highlighted item
- Set a timer for 5 minutes
- Complete only this action, with permission to extend if momentum develops
- Acknowledge completion regardless of outcome

Step 5: Next-step determination (5 minutes)

- Assess current capacity honestly
- Choose one: continue task momentum, address basic needs, seek support, or rest
- Communicate status to necessary others
- Set concrete time parameters for next activity

This 25-minute protocol doesn't solve underlying problems but creates enough temporary stability to make thoughtful decisions instead of reactive ones. It works by addressing the four key components of overwhelm: physiological dysregulation, environmental chaos, attention fragmentation, and initiation paralysis.

The structure matters—following these steps in sequence leverages the way our neurological systems stabilize, moving from basic physiological regulation toward increasingly complex cognitive functions rather than trying to address everything simultaneously.

2. The Capacity Triage System

On particularly challenging days, determining what genuinely needs attention versus what can wait becomes especially difficult. The Capacity Triage System provides a structured approach to making these decisions when overwhelm clouds judgment.

Borrowed from emergency medicine principles, this system categorizes tasks and demands into four levels:

Red Zone: Immediate attention required

- Genuine emergencies affecting physical safety
- Time-sensitive opportunities that won't repeat

- Relationship crises requiring prompt response
- Legal or financial deadlines with significant consequences

Yellow Zone: Important but flexible

- Responsibilities that matter but have some timing flexibility
- Relationship maintenance that strengthens important connections
- Self-care necessary for continued functioning
- Preparation for upcoming red zone items

Green Zone: Beneficial when possible

- Growth opportunities without immediate deadlines
- Nice-to-have improvements to existing systems
- Relationship enrichment beyond basic maintenance
- Activities that build long-term resources

Black Zone: Release and reschedule

- Tasks impossible given current resource limitations
- Commitments based on previous capacity that no longer exists

- Expectations primarily driven by external pressure rather than actual necessity
- Activities that drain resources without proportional benefit

During acute overwhelm, this system helps prioritize where to direct limited attention and energy. Most importantly, it explicitly acknowledges the black zone—items that genuinely cannot be addressed given current limitations and require conscious release rather than persistent guilt.

A quick triage assessment might look like:

1. List everything demanding attention
2. Quickly assign each item a color code
3. Address red zone items first
4. Identify the most important yellow zone item
5. Explicitly communicate about black zone items
6. Reassess as conditions change

This isn't a permanent classification but a dynamic response to current conditions. Items may move between zones as circumstances and capacity fluctuate.

3. The Overwhelm Communication Template

During acute overwhelm, communicating with others about your state and capacity often becomes difficult precisely when it's most necessary. Having pre-formulated language ready for these situations can preserve relationships while protecting limited resources.

Basic Template: "I'm currently experiencing overwhelm due to [brief context if appropriate]. My capacity for [specific function] is temporarily limited. For urgent matters regarding [specific responsibility], please [alternative contact method or person]. For non-urgent items, I'll be able to respond after [timeframe]. Thank you for understanding."

Workplace Example: "I'm currently managing several competing deadlines and need to focus my attention to meet our primary objectives. For the remainder of today, I'll be checking email once at 3pm rather than responding immediately. For anything requiring immediate attention, please text me directly. For other matters, I'll respond during my regular email check-in or tomorrow morning."

Personal Example: "I'm feeling pretty overwhelmed right now and need some time to reset. I care about our conversation and want to give it proper attention. Can we pause for today and continue tomorrow when I'll be more present? I appreciate your understanding."

Family Example: "Today is a high-overwhelm day for me. I can handle essential family needs, but I need to minimize extra demands. I've created a list of what I can realistically manage today on the kitchen whiteboard. For anything else, please either handle independently or save for tomorrow unless truly urgent."

Having these templates ready—perhaps saved in your phone or posted somewhere private—eliminates the need to compose thoughtful communication during states where composition itself is difficult. They protect relationships by clarifying that capacity limitations are temporary rather than reflecting relationship value.

The Surprisingly Effective "Fuck It" Bucket System

While the previous tools address acute overwhelm episodes, managing ongoing apocalypse overwhelm requires more sustainable systems. One particularly effective approach combines psychological wisdom with practical organization: the "Fuck It" Bucket System.

Despite its irreverent name, this system addresses a serious challenge: the psychological drain of carrying too many incomplete responsibilities and open loops simultaneously. Research consistently shows that our minds devote background processing resources to uncompleted tasks even when we're not actively working on them—a phenomenon psychologists call the "Zeigarnik effect."

During apocalyptic times, when both the number and severity of these open loops increase dramatically, this background processing can consume resources needed for immediate functioning. The "Fuck It" Bucket System provides a structured approach to temporarily or permanently liberating these mental resources.

How the System Works

The system creates five distinct "buckets" or categories for organizing responsibilities, tasks, and concerns:

1. The Active Bucket (doing now)

- Contains only items currently receiving direct attention
- Limited to 1-3 items maximum at any given time

- Requires explicit completion criteria for each item
- Focuses exclusively on the specific next action for each item

2. The On-Deck Bucket (doing next)

- Holds items that will move to Active status when current priorities complete
- Limited to 3-5 items maximum
- Requires clear trigger conditions for activation
- Contains only items with genuinely high importance and urgency

3. The Holding Bucket (doing later)

- Stores items acknowledged as important but not time-sensitive
- Organized by category rather than individual tasks
- Reviewed on a regular schedule (weekly/ monthly)
- Protected from constant addition without corresponding removal

4. The Delegation Bucket (someone else is doing)

- Contains responsibilities explicitly transferred to others

- Includes clear documentation of who, what, and when
- Distinguishes between delegated (still your responsibility) and transferred (no longer your responsibility)
- Requires communication protocols for each item

5. The Fuck It Bucket (consciously not doing)

- Holds items explicitly released from obligation
- Distinguished from mere procrastination by conscious decision
- Includes documentation of decision rationale
- Categorized as temporary releases (can be reconsidered later) or permanent releases (genuinely abandoned)

The power of this system comes not just from organization but from the psychological permission to consciously release obligations that exceed current capacity. The explicit "Fuck It" bucket creates legitimate space for acknowledging limitations without the persistent guilt of unarticulated abandonment.

Implementing the System

While the concept is straightforward, effective implementation includes several key components:

1. Physical representation Create tangible representations of each bucket—whether digital or analog—that provide visual feedback on current distribution. Simple options include:

- Labeled folders (physical or digital)
- Board with movable items (physical or virtual)
- Color-coded lists in a single document
- Separate notebooks for each category

The physical manifestation matters because it externalizes decisions that would otherwise consume internal cognitive resources.

2. Regular migration rituals Establish specific times for moving items between buckets, with attention to:

- Daily review of Active and On-Deck buckets
- Weekly review of Holding bucket
- Monthly review of Delegation and Fuck It buckets

These reviews prevent the system from becoming static and unresponsive to changing conditions.

3. Clear criteria for bucket decisions Develop personal guidelines for determining which bucket receives which items, considering:

- Genuine urgency versus perceived pressure
- Alignment with core values and priorities
- Realistic capacity assessment
- Consequences of non-completion
- Resource requirements versus availability

These criteria prevent arbitrary decisions that might increase rather than decrease overwhelm.

4. Communication protocols Establish how bucket decisions affect communication with others, including:

- Standard language for delegation conversations
- Templates for declining or deferring requests
- Notification systems for status changes
- Boundary setting around bucket decisions

Clear communication prevents relationship damage from necessary capacity limitations.

5. Permission practices Develop personal rituals that reinforce the legitimacy of conscious release, such as:

- Written acknowledgment of released obligations
- Conversation with trusted others about difficult releases

- Recognition of capacity preserved through strategic releases
- Gratitude for what remains possible due to conscious limitations

These practices address the guilt that often accompanies necessary boundary setting during overwhelm.

The system's name deliberately uses irreverent language to counteract the excessive seriousness with which we often approach obligations during crisis. The mild shock value of the "Fuck It" label helps interrupt perfectionistic thinking patterns that exacerbate overwhelm rather than relieving it.

Permission to Drop Balls (They Were Never All Staying in the Air Anyway)

Beyond specific systems like the "Fuck It" Bucket, managing apocalypse overwhelm requires a more fundamental permission: acknowledging that during crisis periods, dropping some balls isn't just inevitable but necessary.

The juggling metaphor illustrates this well. When resources diminish and demands increase, attempting to keep all previous balls in the air guarantees a chaotic crash. Strategic decisions about which balls to continue juggling and which to consciously set down creates the possibility of sustainable function instead of total collapse.

The Glass Ball Principle

Not all dropped balls have equal consequences. One useful framework distinguishes between:

Glass balls: When dropped, these shatter with significant, potentially irreversible consequences. Examples include:

- Basic health maintenance
- Core relationship needs
- Essential financial stability
- Fundamental safety requirements
- Primary care responsibilities

Rubber balls: When dropped, these bounce and can be picked up later. Examples include:

- Most work projects and deadlines
- Many social obligations
- Routine maintenance tasks
- Personal development goals
- Non-essential commitments

Paper balls: When dropped, these wrinkle but can be smoothed later if desired. Examples include:

- Aesthetic standards
- Organizational perfection
- Non-critical routines
- Nice-to-have activities
- Status markers and appearances

During apocalyptic times, the number of balls generally increases while juggling capacity decreases. Attempting to preserve the illusion of handling everything inevitably leads to dropping balls randomly rather than strategically—including potentially shattering glass balls that actually matter.

Conscious permission to drop specific balls—particularly rubber and paper ones—protects the capacity needed for glass balls. This isn't failure but strategic resource allocation during constrained conditions.

Identifying Your Specific Balls

The categories above provide general guidance, but specific items vary significantly between individuals based on values, circumstances, and responsibilities. A personalized inventory helps identify which specific balls fall into which categories for your situation:

1. List everything currently demanding attention and resources

2. For each item, ask:

   - What happens if I drop this temporarily?
   - What happens if I drop this permanently?
   - Who besides me is affected by this decision?
   - What resources does maintaining this require?
   - What values does this represent or serve?

3. Based on honest answers, assign each item to a category:

   - Glass: Critical to maintain despite resource constraints
   - Rubber: Important but can be temporarily set aside
   - Paper: Dispensable without significant consequence

4. Review category assignments with consideration for:

   - External versus internal pressures
   - Short-term versus long-term impacts
   - Potential for partial rather than complete dropping
   - Possibility of delegation or renegotiation

This personalized inventory prevents either dropping truly important balls due to poor discernment or maintaining trivial balls at the expense of significant ones.

Managing Others' Expectations

One of the most challenging aspects of strategic ball-dropping is managing others' expectations— particularly those who may not understand your capacity limitations or priority decisions.

Some approaches that help navigate these difficult conversations:

1. **Explicit renegotiation**

Rather than silently dropping balls that affect others, explicitly renegotiate expectations: "Given current circumstances, I need to adjust what I can realistically accomplish. Can we discuss priorities and identify what's genuinely essential versus what could be modified or postponed?"

2. Partial alternatives

Instead of all-or-nothing framing, offer partial alternatives that acknowledge the importance while respecting capacity: "I can't manage the full commitment we initially discussed, but I could contribute in this more limited way. Would that still be helpful, or should we look at other options?"

3. Transparent timelines

Provide clear information about when capacity might change rather than indefinite deferral: "I need to set this aside until [specific date], when I'll reassess. I'll update you then rather than leaving this open-ended."

4. Value acknowledgment

Explicitly recognize the value of what's being set aside to prevent misinterpretation as dismissal: "This matters to me, and ordinarily I would prioritize it. My current need to focus elsewhere doesn't reflect its importance."

5. Mutual problem-solving invitation

Frame capacity limitations as a shared challenge rather than unilateral decision: "Here's the situation I'm facing... I'm struggling to see how to handle everything with my current resources. Do you have thoughts on possible approaches?"

These conversations are rarely easy, but they prevent the relationship damage that comes from either overcommitment followed by failure or silent withdrawal without explanation.

Cognitive Load Management Strategies

Beyond specific tasks and responsibilities, apocalypse overwhelm often involves excessive cognitive load—too many mental processes occurring simultaneously with too few resources to handle them effectively. Managing this cognitive dimension becomes essential for maintaining functionality during crisis periods.

Understanding Cognitive Load Components

Cognitive load consists of three distinct components:

1. **Intrinsic load:** The inherent complexity of tasks or situations requiring attention
2. **Extraneous load:** Additional mental effort required due to how information is presented or processed
3. **Germane load:** Mental resources devoted to creating lasting understanding or skill development

During apocalyptic times, intrinsic load often increases (more complex challenges), while resources for handling extraneous load decrease (due to stress, exhaustion, or disruption).

Effective cognitive load management involves strategic approaches to each component:

Strategies for Reducing Intrinsic Load

While the inherent complexity of apocalyptic challenges can't be eliminated, several approaches can make it more manageable:

1. **Chunking complex situations** Break overwhelming scenarios into smaller, more defined components that can be addressed separately.

2. **Sequential rather than simultaneous processing** Address complex elements in sequence rather than parallel, reducing the concurrent demand on working memory.

3. **Concept mapping for clarity** Create visual representations of complex situations to externalize relationships between elements rather than holding them all in working memory.

4. **Pareto principle application** Identify the 20% of factors likely responsible for 80% of impact, focusing attention on highest-leverage elements.

5. **Complexity thresholds** Establish personal limits for complexity engagement, scheduling regular breaks when dealing with highly complex situations.

These approaches don't simplify the objective complexity but optimize how you engage with it given limited cognitive resources.

Strategies for Minimizing Extraneous Load

Extraneous load—cognitive effort that doesn't contribute to understanding or addressing core challenges—can be significantly reduced through intentional practices:

1. **Information environment design** Create physical and digital environments that minimize unnecessary cognitive demands:

   - Single-task workspaces
   - Notification management
   - Visual simplification
   - Template use for routine decisions
   - Standardized information organization
2. **Decision architecture** Establish systems that reduce decision fatigue:

   - Predefined criteria for common choices
   - Decision trees for repetitive situations
   - Default options for low-consequence decisions
   - Batching similar decisions
   - Elimination of false choices

3. **Attention protection** Implement boundaries around what receives mental focus:

- Scheduled information intake
- Category-based attention allocation
- Time-boxing for high-demand activities
- Distraction elimination during critical tasks
- Task transition buffers

4. **Cognitive offloading** Transfer internal mental processes to external systems:

- Comprehensive documentation rather than memory reliance
- Physical or digital organizing systems
- Calculation and analysis tools
- Reminder and tracking systems
- Delegation of appropriate cognitive tasks

These approaches conserve limited cognitive resources for genuinely necessary processing rather than wasteful extraneous demands.

Strategies for Optimizing Germane Load

During overwhelming periods, resources for learning and growth (germane load) often disappear entirely. Strategic approaches can preserve some capacity for this essential function:

1. **Minimal viable learning** Identify the smallest learning unit that provides meaningful benefit and focus exclusively on that element rather than comprehensive mastery.

2. **Just-in-time skill acquisition** Acquire new knowledge or skills at the point of application rather than in advance, reducing memory demands while increasing relevance.

3. **Experience documentation** Systematically record insights and learnings in external systems to prevent loss during overwhelming periods and enable later integration.

4. **Learning community distribution** Distribute learning across a network rather than individually, with explicit knowledge sharing protocols to reduce redundant effort.

5. **Strategic ignorance designation** Explicitly identify areas where current mastery is

unnecessary, liberating cognitive resources from low-value learning pursuits.

These approaches maintain some capacity for growth and adaptation even during crisis periods, preventing complete stagnation while respecting genuine limitations.

Information Management During Crisis

A significant contributor to apocalypse overwhelm is the unprecedented volume of potentially important information we now encounter daily. During crisis periods, both the quantity and the perceived consequence of information increase dramatically, creating what researcher Alex Edmans calls "information overload with attention underload."

Developing sustainable information management approaches becomes essential for preserving psychological functioning during these periods.

The Three-Tier Information Triage

Not all information requires the same level of engagement. The Three-Tier Information Triage system provides a structured approach to differentiating information based on relevance and actionability:

Tier 1: Need to Know

- Directly affects immediate decisions or safety
- Relates to primary responsibilities
- Requires specific action in a defined timeframe
- Changes fundamental understanding of critical situations

Tier 2: Good to Know

- Provides context for important but not immediate decisions
- Expands understanding of significant situations
- May require action in an undefined future
- Connects to established interests or responsibilities

Tier 3: Peripheral Awareness

- General information without specific action implications
- Background context without immediate relevance

- Potentially interesting but not directly applicable
- Tangentially related to current priorities

During overwhelm periods, this triage allows explicit decisions about engagement level with incoming information:

- Tier 1: Full attention and processing
- Tier 2: Captured for later review
- Tier 3: Brief registration without retention effort

This differentiated approach prevents the common pattern of treating all information as equally demanding of attention—a pattern that guarantees cognitive overwhelm during information-dense crisis periods.

Information Schemas for Efficient Processing

Beyond triage, developing organized frameworks for processing information—what cognitive scientists call "schemas"—significantly reduces the mental effort required to integrate new data.

Some approaches for creating functional information schemas during apocalyptic times:

1. **Situation maps** Visual representations of key factors in complex situations, updated as new information arrives. These externalize mental models, reducing the cognitive load of information integration.

2. **Question frameworks** Sets of consistent questions applied to new information, creating standardized processing pathways:

   ○ How does this change my understanding of [specific situation]?
   ○ What actions, if any, does this suggest or require?
   ○ How reliable is the source and methodology?
   ○ What context might be missing from this information?
   ○ How does this connect to what I already know?

3. **Update protocols** Systematic approaches for modifying existing understanding based on new information:

   ○ Regular designated times for information review

- Templates for documenting significant changes
- Thresholds for when updates warrant immediate attention
- Processes for resolving conflicting information

4. **Source hierarchies** Organized frameworks for evaluating information source reliability:

- Pre-evaluated source categories
- Triangulation requirements for critical information
- Contextual credibility factors
- Expertise domain boundaries

These structured approaches reduce the cognitive burden of information processing during overwhelm periods, preventing both uncritical acceptance and hypervigilant mistrust—both common responses to information overwhelm.

Media Consumption Protocols

Beyond general information management, specific approaches to media consumption become particularly important during apocalyptic times when both the volume and emotional intensity of media increase dramatically.

Effective media consumption protocols might include:

1. **Scheduled intake periods** Designated times for media consumption rather than continuous availability, with clear boundaries before sleep and immediately after waking.

2. **Source limitation** Deliberate restriction to specific, high-quality information sources rather than unlimited browsing, with selection based on signal-to-noise ratio rather than alignment with existing views.

3. **Format diversification** Varied information formats (text, audio, visual, conversation) to prevent medium-specific fatigue and cognitive strain.

4. **Processing pairs** Partnership with others for joint information review, providing multiple perspectives and shared cognitive processing capacity.

5. **Synthesis practices** Regular activities that integrate and contextualize consumed information:

   - Conversation with trusted others
   - Written reflection
   - Explicit connection to existing knowledge
   - Application consideration

These protocols transform media consumption from passive overwhelm to active engagement, reducing the psychological toll of necessary information intake during crisis periods.

The Balance of Action and Acceptance

Perhaps the most challenging aspect of managing apocalypse overwhelm involves navigating the tension between action and acceptance—determining when to strive for change versus when to acknowledge immutable realities. This discernment becomes particularly difficult during crisis, when both unnecessary struggle and premature surrender carry significant costs.

The Serenity Discernment Framework

An expanded version of the familiar serenity prayer offers a practical framework for this discernment:

1. **Things I can control directly** Elements where my individual action creates reliable effects:

    - My own responses and behaviors
    - My immediate environment
    - My information consumption
    - My resource allocation
    - My relationship contributions

2. **Things I can influence but not control** Elements where my action contributes to but doesn't determine outcomes:

    - Some collective decisions
    - Certain relationship dynamics
    - Limited system functions
    - Partial environmental factors
    - Some resource distributions

3. **Things I cannot control or influence** Elements genuinely beyond both control and influence:

    - Global system dynamics

- Others' autonomous choices
- Natural phenomena
- Historical factors
- Certain biological realities

The framework suggests different engagement modes for each category:

- Control zone: Direct action and responsibility
- Influence zone: Strategic intervention and collaborative engagement
- Beyond-influence zone: Radical acceptance and adaptation

Overwhelm often results from misclassification—treating influence zone items as directly controllable (creating frustration) or treating control zone items as beyond influence (creating helplessness).

Practices for Engagement Discernment

Several practices support more accurate classification and appropriate response:

1. **Regular boundary assessment** Periodically reviewing the boundaries between control, influence, and beyond-influence zones, recognizing that these boundaries shift as circumstances and capacities change.

2. **Influence experiments** Small tests to determine whether something initially perceived as beyond influence might actually respond to certain approaches, with careful documentation of results.

3. **Control release rituals** Specific practices for consciously releasing perceived control over items genuinely beyond influence, creating psychological space for more productive focus.

4. **Influence enhancement strategies** Deliberate approaches for expanding influence where possible:

   - Skill development
   - Coalition building
   - Resource pooling
   - Leverage identification
   - Strategic positioning

5. **Acceptance without resignation** Practices that acknowledge current limits without foreclosing future possibilities:

- Distinguishing between present and permanent limitations
- Recognizing cyclical patterns that may create future openings
- Maintaining readiness for unexpected influence opportunities
- Preserving core values even while accepting tactical constraints

These practices prevent both the exhaustion of fighting unwinnable battles and the premature surrender of potentially influential engagement.

Conclusion: The Dance of Overwhelm and Agency

As we conclude this exploration of managing apocalypse overwhelm, it's worth emphasizing that the goal isn't eliminating overwhelm entirely—a probably impossible standard during genuinely overwhelming times. Rather, the aim is developing a sustainable relationship with overwhelm that prevents paralysis without requiring impossible levels of control.

Think of it as learning to dance with overwhelm rather than trying to defeat it. This dance involves constant adjustment, periodic rest, strategic engagement, and authentic acknowledgment of both capability and limitation.

The practices we've explored—from the emergency reset protocol to the "Fuck It" bucket system to cognitive load management—provide concrete steps for this dance. But perhaps most important is the underlying perspective: overwhelming circumstances don't indicate personal failure but appropriate response to genuine conditions.

By developing skills for dancing with overwhelm rather than drowning in it, we maintain our capacity for meaningful engagement even when perfect functioning remains out of reach. We protect our ability to make conscious choices rather than reactive moves. We preserve space for both necessary action and essential acceptance.

In the next chapter, we'll explore another essential apocalyptic skill: maintaining creativity and generative capacity even when circumstances seem to demand constant crisis response.

CHAPTER 12: Creating When the World Is Ending

"But how can I possibly focus on creative work when everything is falling apart?"

I've heard this question countless times from writers, artists, musicians, programmers, designers, and makers of all kinds. It's a question that carries both genuine struggle and implicit guilt—as if continuing to create during crisis somehow indicates insufficient concern about serious matters.

Yet throughout history, humans have continued to create even in the most dire circumstances. Art emerged from concentration camps. Music developed in war zones. Literature blossomed during plagues. Code was written during economic collapse. Design evolved under oppression.

This persistent creativity isn't frivolous or escapist. It's a profound expression of what makes us human—our capacity to generate meaning and beauty even when external conditions seem to render such efforts pointless.

In this chapter, we'll explore practical approaches to maintaining creative capacity during apocalyptic times, not despite our awareness of difficult realities but alongside it. We'll examine how creation functions not merely as distraction but as essential processing tool, meaning-making practice, and act of resistance against forces that would reduce us to mere survival.

Why Making Things Matters Even More During Crisis

Before addressing the how of creativity during apocalyptic times, let's examine the why. What specific functions does creative work serve during periods of crisis that make it worth preserving rather than setting aside until "things settle down"?

Creation as Processing Tool

Neuroscience and psychology research consistently show that creative activities provide unique pathways for processing complex experiences, particularly those involving trauma or significant disruption:

1. **Non-verbal processing channels** Creative modalities—whether visual art, music, movement, or other forms—activate brain regions not accessed through purely verbal processing. This allows integration of experiences that may resist conventional cognitive processing.

2. **Implicit memory exploration** Creativity often accesses implicit memory (unconscious, bodily-stored experience) rather than just explicit memory (conscious narrative recall). During crisis, much experience gets stored implicitly due to overwhelm, making creative approaches particularly valuable for integration.

3. **Metaphorical distance and safety** Creative expression allows exploration of difficult material through metaphor and symbolic

representation, creating psychological safety that enables processing what might otherwise remain too threatening to approach directly.

4. **Bilateral brain activation** Many creative activities involve bilateral brain activation—engagement of both hemispheres—which research suggests is particularly effective for processing traumatic or overwhelming material that might otherwise remain fragmented.

These processing functions make creativity not a luxury during crisis but a sophisticated tool for maintaining psychological integration when conventional meaning-making systems become overwhelmed.

Creation as Meaning-Making Practice

Beyond processing immediate experience, creative work serves essential meaning-making functions during periods when conventional meaning frameworks fail:

1. **Narrative reconstruction** When existing narratives about how the world works

collapse, creative work helps reconstruct sustainable stories that acknowledge disruption while preserving coherence and possibility.

2. **Value embodiment** Creative expression allows concrete manifestation of abstract values, affirming their continued relevance even when external circumstances seem to contradict them.

3. **Order within chaos** The internal logic and structure of creative works provides experiences of coherence and pattern even amid external disorder, satisfying the fundamental human need for comprehensible organization.

4. **Legacy connection** Creative traditions link present experience to both historical precedent and future possibility, contextualizing current disruption within larger temporal frameworks.

These meaning-making functions become particularly important during apocalyptic periods when conventional sources of meaning (stable institutions, predictable futures, shared cultural frameworks) undergo disruption or collapse.

Creation as Resistance

Finally, creative work during crisis serves as resistance to forces that would reduce human experience to mere survival or reaction:

1. **Assertion of agency** Creating asserts that despite external constraints, internal generative capacity remains alive—a profound statement of continued agency amid conditions that might otherwise produce only victimhood or resignation.

2. **Prefigurative practice** Creative work embodies alternative possibilities, demonstrating in microcosm values and approaches that might eventually transform larger systems.

3. **Witness function** Art and other creative forms bear witness to both suffering and resilience in ways that resist erasure or simplification of complex realities.

4. **Pleasure politics** Finding joy and beauty in creative process asserts that pleasure remains legitimate even during difficult times —a countercultural stance when dominant narratives demand either constant alarm or inappropriate positivity.

From this perspective, continuing to create during apocalyptic times constitutes not denial or distraction but deliberate resistance to forces that would diminish the full spectrum of human capacity and expression.

Creativity as Processing Tool, Not Productivity Measure

One of the most common obstacles to sustained creativity during crisis is the conflation of creative process with productivity expectations. When creative practice becomes measured primarily by output metrics—words written, projects completed, audience reached—it often collapses under apocalyptic conditions where such outcomes may become temporarily impossible.

Reframing creativity as processing tool rather than productivity measure creates space for sustainable practice even during extremely challenging periods.

Signs of Productivity-Focused Creativity

How do you know if you've conflated creativity with productivity? Watch for these indicators:

- Evaluating creative sessions primarily by quantifiable output
- Feeling creative work is "pointless" if not working toward finished products
- Abandoning creative practice entirely when completion timelines extend
- Experiencing shame rather than relief after creative sessions without clear outcomes
- Using language like "should," "must," or "have to" around creative work
- Comparing current creative output to pre-crisis levels

- Seeing creative time as justifiable only if it generates tangible results

When these patterns dominate, creativity becomes another demand rather than a resource during difficult times.

Reframing Creative Practice

Several conceptual shifts help transform creativity from productivity measure to processing tool:

1. **Process orientation** Focus primarily on the experience of creating rather than products that may result, asking "How did that feel?" rather than "What did I accomplish?"

2. **Integration metrics** Evaluate creative sessions by processing indicators—emotional release, insight generation, increased clarity, reduced rumination—rather than production metrics.

3. **Expanded purpose recognition** Acknowledge the multiple simultaneous functions of creative work—psychological integration, skill maintenance, joy generation,

meaning connection—rather than single-purpose output focus.

4. **Timeframe extension** Adopt extended or indefinite timeframes for completion that accommodate crisis conditions rather than imposing pre-crisis expectations on apocalyptic circumstances.

5. **Documentation rather than evaluation** Replace judgmental assessment of creative work with curious documentation of what emerged, treating all creative artifacts as information rather than achievements or failures.

These reframes create space for creativity to function as processing tool even when productivity in conventional terms becomes temporarily impossible.

Practical Implementation Approaches

Moving from conceptual reframing to practical implementation might include:

1. **Process journaling** Maintain a record focused exclusively on creative experience rather than outcomes, documenting internal shifts, interesting moments, or surprising discoveries regardless of "productive" results.

2. **Time-based rather than output-based goals** Structure creative practice around time engaged rather than production targets: "I'll spend 20 minutes with this project" instead of "I'll finish this section today."

3. **Integration pauses** Include explicit reflection moments during and after creative sessions focused on what you're learning, processing, or integrating through the creative engagement.

4. **Multi-purpose acknowledgment** Begin creative sessions by explicitly naming multiple valid purposes beyond productivity: "Today this might generate insight, provide enjoyment, maintain skills, or process emotions—all are welcome."

5. **Artifact relationship shifts** Develop language and practices that honor creative artifacts as temporary processing tools rather than permanent representations of capability: "This reflects where I am today" rather than "This shows what I can do."

These practical approaches support sustained creative engagement even when conventional productivity becomes difficult or impossible due to crisis conditions.

Finding Inspiration in Unlikely Disaster Scenarios

Beyond reframing creativity itself, apocalyptic times often require finding new sources of inspiration when conventional wells run dry. Counterintuitively, the very conditions that seem to render creativity impossible sometimes contain unique inspirational possibilities unavailable during more stable periods.

Crisis-Specific Inspiration Sources

Several inspiration sources become particularly accessible during apocalyptic times:

1. **Boundary dissolution** Crisis often dissolves boundaries between previously separated domains—work/home, public/private, body/environment—creating unique juxtapositions that generate creative tension and possibility.

2. **Heightened awareness** Survival-level vigilance during crisis can produce unusually acute observation and perception, providing access to sensory and emotional detail that might go unnoticed during more routine periods.

3. **Value clarification** When non-essentials fall away due to crisis constraints, core values often emerge with unusual clarity, providing potent creative material connected to fundamental rather than superficial concerns.

4. **System revelation** Breakdowns in normally invisible systems reveal mechanisms and interconnections typically hidden from view, offering unprecedented insight into how

things actually work versus how they're portrayed.

5. **Temporal distortion** Crisis-induced alterations in time perception—whether compression or expansion—create unique perspectives on sequence, causality, and relationship that can fuel creative exploration.

These crisis-specific sources often generate creative material with unusual depth and resonance precisely because they emerge from genuine engagement with significant experience rather than manufactured artistic premises.

Accessing Crisis-Specific Inspiration

Specific practices can help access these unique inspiration sources:

1. **Boundary mapping** Document where previously solid boundaries between domains have become permeable or dissolved, exploring the creative potential in these new intersections.

2. **Sensory inventory** Conduct regular detailed inventories of sensory experience during crisis, noting elements that seem particularly heightened, altered, or newly significant.

3. **Value clarification exercises** Explicitly identify which values emerge as non-negotiable during crisis versus which reveal themselves as contextual or optional, using this clarification as creative foundation.

4. **System tracing** When encountering system breakdowns, trace the revealed connections and mechanisms with curiosity rather than just frustration, documenting insights about previously invisible operations.

5. **Temporal notation** Keep records of how time perception alters during crisis—moments of unusual expansion or compression, disrupted sequences, collapsed or extended durations —as material for creative exploration.

These practices transform crisis conditions from obstacles to creativity into unique sources of insight and inspiration unavailable during more stable periods.

Creating with Constrained Resources

Apocalyptic times typically involve significant resource constraints—reduced time, energy, money, space, materials, or attention. Rather than abandoning creative practice until constraints ease, adapting to work effectively within limitations often generates surprising creative breakthroughs.

The Generative Potential of Constraints

Contrary to romantic notions of unlimited freedom as creativity's ideal condition, research consistently shows that appropriate constraints often enhance rather than inhibit creative output:

1. **Focus amplification** Constraints direct limited attention to specific elements rather than dissipating across too many possibilities, creating depth rather than diffusion.

2. **Invention necessity** Resource limitations require innovative approaches that might never emerge under conditions of abundance.

3. **Essence clarification** Constraints force identification of what's truly essential versus optional in any creative undertaking, often distilling more powerful expressions.

4. **Productive friction** The resistance created by limitations generates creative tension that conventional approaches often lack, producing energy rather than merely consuming it.

Understanding this generative potential transforms constraints from creativity obstacles to creativity catalysts, particularly relevant during apocalyptic periods when constraints multiply.

Practical Approaches to Constraint-Based Creativity

Several approaches support effective creative practice under significant constraints:

1. **Constraint inventory** Begin by explicitly identifying current constraints rather than working against unacknowledged limitations. Categories might include:

    - Time (when/how much is actually available)
    - Energy (peak capacity periods and limitations)
    - Space (physical and psychological working conditions)
    - Materials (what remains accessible vs. what's unavailable)
    - Attention (focus capacity and common interruptions)
    - Support (available vs. unavailable assistance)

2. **Minimum viable creative unit** Identify the smallest complete creative unit that provides satisfaction and maintains practice:

- For writers: Perhaps a single paragraph rather than a chapter
- For musicians: A 30-second phrase rather than complete composition
- For visual artists: A thumbnail sketch rather than finished piece
- For designers: A core concept rather than detailed execution
- For coders: A single function rather than complete feature

3. **Time concentration practices** Develop approaches that concentrate available time into focused rather than fragmented periods:

- Creative sprints (5-15 minutes of complete focus)
- Transition rituals (rapid entry into creative mindset)
- Continuation markers (clear documentation of where to resume)
- Portable tools (materials accessible in various environments)
- Compound time aggregation (accumulating tiny sessions into larger work)

4. **Modular creation frameworks** Design creative projects with modular architecture that accommodates intermittent engagement:

- Self-contained components that retain value independently
- Non-linear structures allowing work in any sequence
- Scalable scope adjustable to available resources
- Multiple completion thresholds at different investment levels
- Discrete elements combinable in various configurations

5. **Collaborative resource pooling** Develop structures for sharing limited resources across multiple creators:

- Shared workspaces (physical or digital)
- Material exchanges
- Skill swaps
- Attention/feedback pools
- Completion partnerships

These approaches don't eliminate the reality of constraints but transform their relationship to creative practice, allowing continued engagement even under significant limitation.

Navigating Creative Blocks Specific to Crisis

Beyond general resource constraints, apocalyptic times often generate specific creative blocks that require targeted approaches. Understanding and addressing these particular obstacles helps maintain creative capacity during periods when conventional unblocking techniques may prove insufficient.

Crisis-Specific Creative Blocks

Several creative blocks appear with particular frequency during apocalyptic periods:

1. **Relevance doubt** The persistent question "How can this possibly matter given everything happening?" that undermines creative engagement by suggesting irrelevance compared to crisis concerns.

2. **Moral paralysis** The sense that creating anything other than direct crisis response represents moral failure or inappropriate prioritization during emergency.

3. **Future absence** The difficulty imagining any audience, purpose, or context for creative work when futures themselves seem radically uncertain or foreclosed.

4. **Premature instrumentalization** The pressure to justify all creative work through immediate practical utility rather than intrinsic value or longer-term significance.

5. **Apocalyptic absorption** The consuming nature of crisis information and response that leaves insufficient internal space for generative thought or expression.

These blocks differ from general creative obstacles in their specific connection to crisis conditions and often prove resistant to conventional unblocking approaches.

Targeted Responses to Crisis Blocks

Each crisis-specific block requires particular strategies for effective navigation:

For relevance doubt:

- Historical contextualization of creative work during previous crises
- Explicit articulation of multiple simultaneous values beyond immediate utility
- Documentation of personal benefit regardless of external impact
- Connection to maintaining human cultural continuity through disruption
- Recognition of creation as meaning-making rather than distraction

For moral paralysis:

- Ethical frameworks for resource allocation that include regenerative practices
- Models of sustainable activism that incorporate creative replenishment
- Clear boundaries between necessary rest and actual avoidance
- Connection to historical traditions that maintain creativity alongside resistance
- Integration of creative practice into rather than separate from response

For future absence:

- Creation focused on present witness rather than future reception

- Documentation-oriented approaches emphasizing record rather than projection
- Connection to cyclical rather than linear time frameworks
- Traditions of creating for unknown futures throughout history
- Heritage-based creative practices that link past, present, and possible futures

For premature instrumentalization:

- Explicit value frameworks beyond immediate utility
- Protection of exploration spaces without predetermined outcomes
- Historical examples of seemingly "useless" creation later proving vital
- Regular practice detached from product orientation
- Integration metrics independent of instrumental value

For apocalyptic absorption:

- Structured information diets with protected creative periods
- Deliberate cultivation of attention diversity beyond crisis focus
- Creation as processing tool for rather than escape from apocalyptic content

- Designated spaces (physical or temporal) free from crisis input
- Social agreements supporting creative engagement alongside response

These targeted approaches address the specific mechanisms of crisis-related creative blocks rather than applying generic creativity advice that often proves insufficient during apocalyptic periods.

Connecting Creation to Larger Purpose

While reframing creativity as process rather than product proves helpful, many people still need connection to purpose beyond immediate experience to sustain creative practice during crisis. Rather than abandonning purpose orientation entirely, expanding and diversifying purpose frameworks supports sustained engagement when conventional goals become temporarily unreachable.

Beyond Individual Achievement

During apocalyptic times, purpose frameworks focused primarily on individual achievement often collapse under conditions where such achievement becomes impossible or seems trivial compared to larger concerns. Alternative purpose frameworks might include:

1. **Witnessing function** Creating as bearing witness to both crisis realities and continued humanity amid disruption—a historically vital function regardless of audience size or immediate impact.

2. **Skill preservation** Creative practice as maintaining capabilities that may serve vital functions in unknown futures rather than immediate contexts.

3. **Cultural continuity** Creation as maintaining threads of human expression through difficult periods, connecting past traditions to future possibilities regardless of present circumstances.

4. **Meaning resistance** Creative work as deliberate resistance to meaning collapse during periods when conventional meaning

frameworks undergo severe disruption.

5. **Community resource generation** Creation as producing potential resources for community sustenance beyond individual benefit or recognition.

These expanded purpose frameworks situate creative work within larger contexts less vulnerable to disruption than individual achievement metrics while maintaining genuine connection to meaningful engagement.

Practical Purpose Connection

Moving from conceptual frameworks to practical implementation might include:

1. **Legacy documentation** Maintaining records explicitly connecting current creative work to both historical precedents and potential futures:

   ○ Historical examples of similar work during crisis periods

- Documentation of process and insights independent of outcomes
- Seeds planted for unknown future conditions
- Connections to traditions that survived previous disruptions
- Explicit naming of values being preserved through practice

2. **Contribution structures** Developing concrete structures for creative work to contribute beyond individual achievement:

- Community archives
- Skill-sharing frameworks
- Resource pooling systems
- Intergenerational transmission methods
- Distributed documentation approaches

3. **Meaning collectives** Creating intentional groups focused on shared meaning-making rather than individual production:

- Creation circles with explicit meaning-maintenance purpose
- Collaborative exploration of specific questions or themes
- Preservation partnerships for particular traditions or approaches

- Mutual witnessing structures for creative process
- Exchange systems for insights and discoveries

4. **Value clarification practices** Regular activities that identify and articulate core values expressed through creative work:

- Value journaling connected to creative sessions
- Periodic review of how values manifest across projects
- Explicit naming of what specific work preserves or expresses
- Connection of personal values to broader cultural valuation
- Articulation of tensions between competing values

These practical approaches transform abstract purpose connection into concrete practices that support sustained creative engagement even when conventional achievement becomes temporarily impossible.

Finding Creative Community During Crisis

While some creative practices can be sustained individually, most creators benefit significantly from community connection—a resource often disrupted during apocalyptic periods due to physical isolation, resource competition, or system breakdown. Developing alternative forms of creative community becomes essential for sustained practice during extended crisis.

Crisis-Adapted Creative Community Models

Several community structures show particular resilience during crisis periods:

1. **Micro-communities** Very small groups (2-5 people) requiring minimal coordination and resource investment while providing essential feedback, accountability, and witnessing functions.

2. **Asynchronous exchange networks** Non-simultaneous sharing systems that accommodate disrupted schedules and capacity fluctuations while maintaining connection through cumulative rather than simultaneous interaction.

3. **Resource pooling collectives** Groups organized explicitly around sharing limited resources—space, materials, skills, attention, feedback—to create sufficiency through exchange rather than individual acquisition.

4. **Documentation circles** Communities focused primarily on witnessing and recording creative process rather than evaluating or improving outputs, preserving the social dimension of creativity without performance pressure.

5. **Tradition maintenance groups** Collectives organized around preserving specific creative traditions through disruption, providing purpose beyond individual expression while connecting to historical continuity.

These alternative models provide essential social dimensions of creativity while requiring fewer resources and less coordination than conventional creative communities.

Practical Implementation Approaches

Moving from models to implementation might include:

1. **Minimal viable community practices** Identifying the smallest sustainable community structures that provide essential creative support:

   - One consistent witness for process rather than multiple critiquers
   - Brief check-ins replacing extended workshops
   - Rotating facilitation to distribute organizational load
   - Deliberately bounded expectations and commitments
   - Explicit discussion of actual versus ideal capacity

2. **Resilient connection methods** Developing communication approaches that function despite disruption:

   - Multiple platform options for various access conditions
   - Low-bandwidth alternatives when digital connection falters

- Physical exchange systems when digital access fails
- Alternating synchronous and asynchronous interaction
- Flexible participation expectations accommodating fluctuating capacity

3. **Explicit resource agreements** Clear frameworks for sharing limited creative resources:

   - Space-sharing protocols (physical or digital)
   - Material exchange systems
   - Skill-sharing arrangements
   - Attention/feedback exchange agreements
   - Time banking for creative support

4. **Meaning-oriented interactions** Community structures focused on shared meaning rather than critique or improvement:

   - Witness circles with suspended evaluation
   - Value articulation exchanges
   - Process documentation sharing
   - Question exploration rather than answer provision

- ○ Meaning resonance rather than quality assessment

These practical approaches transform abstract community models into concrete structures that support creative continuity with minimal resources during crisis periods.

Creating Without Requiring "Feeling Creative"

One of the most common creativity obstacles during apocalyptic times is the absence of "feeling creative"—the subjective sense of inspiration or generative energy that many mistakenly believe must precede creative engagement. Developing approaches that function without requiring this feeling becomes essential for sustained practice during extended crisis.

The Feeling/Function Distinction

Research consistently shows that creative practice can remain functional and valuable even when subjective creative feelings are absent. Understanding this distinction helps prevent abandoning creative engagement during periods when emotional overwhelm, stress response, or traumatic impact temporarily suppress the subjective experience of creativity.

Several key insights support this distinction:

1. **Action precedes feeling** Neurological evidence suggests creative feelings often follow rather than precede creative engagement, emerging from the activity itself rather than serving as necessary prerequisite.

2. **Functional independence** Studies of professional creatives across disciplines reveal that sustainable practice depends on functional approaches independent of subjective state, with consistent engagement regardless of fluctuating feelings.

3. **State irrelevance for certain benefits** Many benefits of creative practice—skill maintenance, processing function, witnessing capacity—occur regardless of subjective creative feeling during the activity.

4. **Temporary versus permanent absence**
Research on creativity during trauma and crisis suggests that subjective creative feelings typically return eventually when practice continues, while abandoning practice can permanently suppress their re-emergence.

These insights support approaches that maintain creative function even during periods when creative feelings temporarily disappear due to crisis conditions.

Feeling-Independent Creative Approaches

Several practical approaches support creative engagement without requiring subjective creative feelings:

1. **Process protocols** Clearly defined step-by-step procedures that function regardless of emotional state:

   ○ Writing: Sentence starter → response → extension → revision

- Visual art: Shape placement → color addition → texture development → integration
- Music: Rhythm definition → tone selection → pattern extension → variation
- Design: Function listing → constraint mapping → option generation → refinement
- Code: Function definition → component development → integration → testing

2. **Environmental triggers** External cues that initiate creative engagement without requiring internal motivation:

- Physical spaces designated exclusively for creative work
- Temporal boundaries that activate practice regardless of state
- Sensory anchors (specific sounds, scents, objects) that initiate creative mode
- Transition rituals that bridge between non-creative and creative states
- Social prompts that activate creative engagement through commitment

3. **Mechanical initiators** Beginning methods that require minimal activation energy:

- Copying existing content before original generation
- Physical engagement preceding conceptual development
- Extremely constrained initial parameters
- Deliberate imitation as starting point
- Template-based rather than blank-slate approaches

4. **Non-creation creative maintenance**
Activities that preserve creative capacity without requiring generation:

- Organizing existing creative materials
- Documentation of past creative processes
- Skill-specific technical practice
- Creative input without output expectation
- Tool maintenance and preparation

These approaches maintain creative function during periods when subjective creative feelings become temporarily inaccessible due to crisis conditions, preventing permanent capacity loss due to practice abandonment.

Conclusion: Creating as Radical Act of Continuation

As we conclude this exploration of creative practice during apocalyptic times, it's worth emphasizing the profound significance of continued creation amid conditions that seem to render it impossible or irrelevant.

Throughout human history, the persistence of creative expression during our darkest periods has never been merely decorative or escapist. It has functioned as essential meaning preservation, psychological integration, cultural continuity, and radical assertion of continued humanity despite forces that would reduce us to mere survival.

The approaches we've explored—from reframing creativity as process rather than product to developing crisis-specific inspiration sources to building resilient creative communities—aren't just coping mechanisms for diminished circumstances. They're sophisticated strategies for maintaining one of our most essential human capacities during periods when that capacity faces its greatest threats.

Creating when the world seems to be ending isn't denial of reality but engagement with its fullest dimensions—acknowledging both the genuine losses and constraints of crisis and the persistent human capacity to generate meaning, beauty, and possibility even within those constraints.

In this light, continuing to create during apocalyptic times becomes not a trivial side activity but a radical act of continuation—asserting through practice that even when much is being lost, our fundamental capacity to make meaning and generate newness remains alive.

This continuation doesn't require grand achievements or perfect conditions. It can manifest in the smallest creative acts undertaken with awareness of their significance—a poem written between crisis responses, a song composed in fragments during brief moments of respite, a design sketched while waiting for emergency information, a line of code written before dawn.

Each of these acts, however humble, maintains the thread of human creativity through the eye of the apocalyptic needle—preserving not just skills or products but the essential human capacity to imagine and manifest worlds beyond the immediate circumstances, no matter how challenging those circumstances become.

In the next chapter, we'll explore how these individual practices connect to larger collective responses—how personal apocalypse navigation can contribute to shared efforts toward more just and sustainable futures beyond current crises.

PART V: THE BIGGER PICTURE

CHAPTER 13: Collective Care in Collapse

So far in this book, we've focused primarily on individual strategies for navigating apocalyptic times—personal practices that help maintain wellbeing despite challenging circumstances. While these approaches provide essential support, focusing exclusively on individual resilience creates two significant problems.

First, it places impossible expectations on individuals to solve systemic problems through personal adaptation. When collective systems fail, no amount of individual resilience can fully compensate. Second, it obscures one of our most powerful resources for navigating crisis: our capacity for collective care and mutual support.

In this chapter, we'll explore how to move beyond purely individual approaches into collective care strategies that multiply resource availability, distribute burdens more equitably, and create sustainability beyond what any person could achieve alone. This isn't about abandoning personal practices but embedding them within wider networks of reciprocal support.

Moving Beyond Self-Care into Community Solutions

The concept of "self-care" emerged from Black feminist activist traditions as a political act of self-preservation within oppressive systems. As Audre Lorde famously wrote, "Caring for myself is not self-indulgence, it is self-preservation, and that is an act of political warfare."

However, as self-care entered mainstream culture, it often transformed into individualistic consumer practices disconnected from systemic analysis or community context. During apocalyptic times, this narrow version of self-care proves woefully insufficient. No individual bubble bath, meditation practice, or wellness product can adequately address the magnitude of systemic challenges we face.

Moving toward collective care involves several key shifts in perspective and practice:

From Individual to Systemic Analysis

Collective care begins with recognizing that many challenges we experience as personal failures or individual burdens actually reflect systemic conditions affecting numerous people simultaneously:

- What appears as personal burnout often reflects unsustainable workloads distributed across entire sectors
- What feels like individual financial struggle often reflects structural economic inequities
- What manifests as personal health challenges often connects to environmental degradation or healthcare access issues
- What presents as family stress often reflects lack of social support infrastructure for care responsibilities

This systemic perspective doesn't dismiss personal experience but contextualizes it within larger patterns, revealing opportunities for collective rather than merely individual response.

From Scarcity to Resource Pooling

Individual approaches often assume fixed resource limitations, with each person working within their separate constraints. Collective care recognizes that pooling resources—whether material, emotional, informational, or temporal—can create sufficiency where individual allocation would produce scarcity.

Examples of effective resource pooling during collapse include:

- **Time banks**: Systems for exchanging time and skills without monetary intermediation
- **Care collectives**: Shared responsibility for dependents (children, elders, those with illness or disability)
- **Tool libraries**: Communal ownership of occasionally-needed items
- **Skill sharing networks**: Distributed expertise accessibility
- **Food sharing systems**: Collective food acquisition and preparation

- **Housing partnerships**: Shared living spaces or housing security collectives

These approaches don't require abundance but create resilience through strategic resource redistribution and creative allocation.

From Competitive to Collaborative Safety

Individual safety-seeking during crisis often becomes competitive—fighting for limited supplies, opportunities, or security at others' expense. Collective care approaches recognize that sustainable safety requires collaborative rather than competitive approaches.

Research consistently shows that communities practicing mutual aid during disasters experience better outcomes than those relying on individual household preparation alone. This collaborative safety operates through several mechanisms:

- **Distributed monitoring**: More eyes watching for threats means earlier detection and response
- **Complementary preparation**: Different people preparing for different contingencies creates broader coverage

- **Response diversity**: Varied skills and resources enable more adaptable crisis response
- **Recovery redundancy**: Multiple support systems create backup when primary systems fail
- **Enhanced meaning framework**: Collective purpose sustains effort beyond what individual survival alone can motivate

Rather than weakening individual security, these collaborative approaches often strengthen it by embedding personal safety within more resilient collective systems.

From Independence to Interdependence

Perhaps most fundamentally, collective care requires shifting from valorizing independence to recognizing interdependence as our actual condition. No human survives or thrives in isolation. Our wellbeing has always depended on complex webs of relationship and exchange.

Apocalyptic conditions don't create this interdependence but often reveal it by disrupting the systems that previously obscured it. When supply chains falter, infrastructure fails, or institutions collapse, the underlying reality of our interdependence becomes unavoidably apparent.

Collective care approaches this interdependence not as weakness to transcend but as reality to work with skillfully—designing systems that acknowledge and support the mutual dependency that has always characterized human survival and flourishing.

Small Ways to Help Others Without Depleting Yourself

While systemic perspective and collective orientation provide essential foundations, many people hesitate to engage with collective care due to legitimate concerns about personal capacity. During apocalyptic times, when individual resources often become severely constrained, the prospect of taking on additional responsibilities for others' wellbeing can seem impossible.

Effective collective care acknowledges these constraints, developing approaches that contribute meaningfully to others without depleting already limited personal resources. The goal isn't sacrificial giving but sustainable reciprocity that ultimately supports everyone involved.

The Capacity-Based Contribution Approach

Rather than one-size-fits-all expectations, capacity-based contribution adapts involvement to individual circumstances, focusing on what each person can sustainably offer rather than what ideally "should" be provided:

1. **Micro-contributions** Small, discrete actions requiring minimal resources but providing genuine value:

   - Text check-ins with vulnerable community members
   - Information sharing that prevents duplicate research efforts
   - Brief skill-specific assistance in areas of personal expertise
   - Resource connection (linking needs with available resources)
   - Witness function (simply being present for difficult experiences)

2. **Intermittent involvement** Periodic rather than continuous engagement matched to fluctuating capacity:

   - Once-weekly rather than daily responsibilities

- Backup roles activated only during specific circumstances
- Seasonal rather than year-round commitments
- Capacity-based scheduling with clear boundaries
- Explicit on/off periods rather than indefinite availability

3. **Leverage-focused engagement** Activities with multiplication effects beyond the initial resource investment:

- System creation that continues functioning with minimal maintenance
- Knowledge transfer that enables others' independent action
- Template development that reduces future effort requirements
- Connection facilitation that generates ongoing relationships
- Infrastructure investment with extended impact duration

4. **Alignment with existing activities** Contributions incorporated into necessary personal activities rather than requiring additional time:

- Shopping for a neighbor while doing personal shopping
- Information gathering that serves both individual and collective needs
- Skill development simultaneously benefiting self and others
- Communication that addresses multiple purposes concurrently
- Transportation sharing during necessary personal travel

5. **Recovery-incorporated contributions**
   Helping activities that simultaneously support personal restoration:

   - Nature-based assistance that provides restoration benefits
   - Social contributions that meet personal connection needs
   - Physical helping that provides needed movement
   - Creative assistance that engages personal creative needs
   - Teaching that reinforces personal knowledge integration

These capacity-based approaches transform helping from depleting obligation to sustainable engagement, matching contribution to actual resources rather than abstract ideals.

Contribution without Saviorism

Another obstacle to healthy collective care involves savior dynamics—approaches that position some as rescuers and others as helpless recipients. These dynamics undermine genuine reciprocity, creating unsustainable hierarchies and reinforcing harmful power imbalances.

Several practical approaches help avoid these pitfalls:

1. **Need normalization** Frameworks that recognize needs as universal human experiences rather than individual deficiencies:

    ◦ Explicit acknowledgment of universal vulnerability
    ◦ Systems designed for everyone's participation as both giver and receiver
    ◦ Language that destigmatizes help-seeking
    ◦ Structures normalizing resource requests

- Celebration of interdependence rather than self-sufficiency

2. **Asset identification** Approaches that recognize everyone's capacity to contribute regardless of circumstance:

  - Skills and resource inventories including non-traditional assets
  - Contribution systems accessible to diverse abilities
  - Recognition of varied contribution forms beyond material assistance
  - Explicit valuation of intangible contributions (emotional support, wisdom sharing, etc.)
  - Systems design incorporating diverse participation modes

3. **Power-conscious practice** Methods that acknowledge and address power differentials rather than ignoring them:

  - Transparent decision-making structures
  - Rotation of leadership/coordination roles
  - Explicit discussion of privilege impacts on contribution capacity

- Accountability systems for power abuse prevention
- Regular power distribution assessment and adjustment

4. **Distributed expertise recognition**
Approaches that value diverse knowledge forms rather than privileging conventional expertise:

- Explicit acknowledgment of experience-based wisdom
- Systems incorporating both credentialed and non-credentialed knowledge
- Decision-making that integrates multiple knowing modes
- Recognition of contextual rather than universal expertise
- Valuation of practical alongside theoretical knowledge

These approaches transform collective care from hierarchical charity to genuine mutual aid, creating sustainability through reciprocity rather than dependency.

Building Care Networks from Scratch

While some people maintain existing communities into apocalyptic times, many face the challenge of building care networks from scratch due to relocation, relationship disruption, or system collapse. Creating new collective care structures during crisis presents unique challenges but remains possible with strategic approaches.

The Micro-Network Starting Point

Rather than attempting immediately to create comprehensive care communities, beginning with small, focused micro-networks often proves more feasible during crisis conditions:

1. **Dyadic partnerships** Two-person mutual support agreements provide maximum simplicity with significant benefit:

   - Check-in partnerships (regular wellbeing confirmation)
   - Skill-exchange pairs (complementary capability sharing)
   - Resource-backup agreements (emergency support arrangements)
   - Information-sharing partnerships (distributed monitoring systems)
   - Emotional support exchanges (scheduled witnessing relationships)

2. **Triangular micro-communities** Three-person networks create stability beyond pairs while maintaining simplicity:

   - Backup redundancy when one person reaches capacity limits
   - Broader skill/resource coverage than dyadic arrangements
   - Simple coordination requiring minimal communication infrastructure
   - Relationship diversity creating resilience beyond single connections
   - Manageable size for initial trust development during crisis

3. **Functional pods** Small groups (4-7 people) organized around specific shared needs:

   - Childcare collectives
   - Elder support circles
   - Food acquisition/preparation groups
   - Transportation sharing arrangements
   - Healthcare monitoring networks

These micro-networks provide immediate mutual aid benefits while potentially serving as building blocks for larger systems as capacity and circumstances permit.

Network Growth through Federation

As initial micro-networks stabilize, federation rather than expansion often provides the most sustainable growth pathway:

1. **Spoke-hub arrangements** Connections between micro-networks through designated points of contact rather than attempting full integration:

   - Inter-network coordination through single representatives
   - Resource sharing through specific exchange protocols
   - Information distribution through designated communication nodes
   - Cross-network skills access through formal request processes
   - Emergency support through predetermined activation pathways

2. **Functional specialization** Networks developing distinct capacities that complement rather than duplicate each other:

   - Different groups focusing on specific resource areas

- Complementary skill development across networks
- Distributed tool/equipment investment
- Varied schedule coverage across groups
- Complementary relationship with formal support systems

3. **Multi-scale organization** Systems operating simultaneously at different scales for different functions:

- Intimate care at micro-network level
- Resource acquisition at mid-level federation
- Advocacy/system engagement at macro-network scale
- Information distribution across multiple levels
- Emergency response coordination at appropriate scale for specific challenges

These federated approaches prevent both the fragility of isolated micro-networks and the complexity burden of attempting comprehensive large-scale organization during crisis conditions.

Building on Existing Infrastructure

Rather than creating wholly new structures, identifying and adapting existing social infrastructure often provides efficient pathways to functional care networks:

1. **Hyper-local geographic units**
   Neighborhood-based organizations adapted for mutual aid:

   - Block associations repurposed for care coordination
   - Apartment building communities activated for resource sharing
   - Neighborhood messaging systems repurposed for needs communication
   - Local gathering spaces converted to mutual aid centers
   - Walkable-distance networks organized for physical resource exchange

2. **Affinity organization adaptation** Existing interest-based groups expanded to include care functions:

   - Religious communities developing explicit mutual aid systems
   - Hobby groups incorporating resource/ skill sharing

- Professional networks adapting for wider support functions
- Cultural organizations expanding into care coordination
- Political groups developing direct mutual aid components

3. **Institutional partnership** Formal organizational relationships supporting informal care networks:

- Library partnerships providing information/space resources
- School connections facilitating family-to-family support
- Healthcare institution relationships supporting community care
- Municipal service coordination with informal networks
- Non-profit organization resources supporting community initiatives

These approaches leverage existing social capital and organizational structures rather than attempting to build entirely new systems during already-challenging circumstances.

Finding Purpose in Being Useful (Without Martyr Complex)

Beyond practical arrangements, sustainable collective care requires addressing the psychological dimensions of helping relationships —particularly finding meaningful purpose through contribution without developing unhealthy martyr dynamics that ultimately undermine both individual wellbeing and collective sustainability.

The Purpose-Wellbeing Connection

Research consistently shows that contributing to others' wellbeing correlates with numerous psychological benefits, including:

- Increased meaning and purpose perception
- Greater life satisfaction
- Reduced depression symptoms
- Enhanced sense of agency and efficacy
- Stronger social connection and belonging

However, these benefits emerge only when helping occurs within sustainable boundaries. When contribution crosses into self-sacrifice or martyrdom, both helper wellbeing and relationship quality typically deteriorate.

Signs of Unsustainable Helping Patterns

Several indicators suggest helping has crossed from sustainable contribution into potential martyrdom:

- Persistent resentment despite continued helping
- Physical symptoms emerging during or after caregiving
- Helping that consistently violates stated boundaries
- Contribution that requires denying basic personal needs
- Assistance motivated primarily by guilt or obligation
- Help that creates provider depletion rather than energy
- Helping relationships marked by increasing asymmetry over time

These patterns indicate helping that ultimately undermines both individual and collective wellbeing rather than enhancing it.

Frameworks for Sustainable Contribution

Several conceptual frameworks support finding genuine purpose through helping while preventing martyr dynamics:

1. **The oxygen mask principle** Just as airplane safety instructions direct securing your own oxygen before assisting others, sustainable collective care requires maintaining personal wellbeing sufficiently to continue contributing effectively.

   This isn't selfish but practical—preserving the resources necessary for ongoing assistance rather than creating helpers who themselves require rescue due to depletion.

2. **The relationship bank account** Viewing helping relationships as accounts requiring both deposits and withdrawals rather than one-way transfers. This framework recognizes that all participants periodically need both to give and to receive.

   Sustainable collective care involves balance over time rather than perfect equality in every interaction. Sometimes you give more; sometimes you receive more—with overall reciprocity emerging through ongoing relationship rather than transaction-by-transaction accounting.

3. **The renewable energy model** Distinguishing between helping that generates renewable energy versus depleting limited reserves. Some forms of contribution actually replenish psychological resources through meaning, connection, and efficacy experiences, while others consistently consume more energy than they generate.

    Sustainable collective care emphasizes the former whenever possible, recognizing that sometimes high-cost helping remains necessary but requires deliberate replenishment strategies.

4. **The shared power perspective** Viewing helping not as rescuing powerless others but as resource sharing among differently situated equals. This framework acknowledges that power differentials exist while rejecting characterizations of some people as solely helpers and others as solely recipients.

Sustainable collective care involves mutual recognition of each person's agency, capacity, and inherent value regardless of circumstance.

Practical Applications for Sustainable Purpose

Moving from conceptual frameworks to practical application involves several specific approaches:

1. **Contribution clarity practices** Regular reflection on personal helping motivations and impacts:

   - Honest assessment of whether specific helping generates or depletes energy
   - Clear articulation of sustainable contribution boundaries
   - Regular evaluation of helping-related resentment as boundary indicator
   - Explicit identification of personal needs requiring attention
   - Periodic review of helping patterns for sustainability

2. **Reciprocity structures** Systems that formalize the expectation that everyone both

gives and receives:

- Scheduled role rotations in care communities
- Explicit need expression encouragement for all participants
- Documentation systems tracking contribution diversity
- Celebration of receiving as community contribution
- Regular participation assessment in multiple roles

3. **Regenerative helping choices** Strategic selection of contribution forms that support helper wellbeing:

- Helping aligned with personal values and strengths
- Contribution with clear positive impact visibility
- Assistance incorporating personal growth opportunities
- Helping that includes connection satisfying relationship needs
- Contribution providing structure and purpose during difficult times

4. **Replenishment rituals** Explicit practices acknowledging and addressing the costs of necessary high-demand helping:

    - Scheduled breaks from care responsibilities
    - Community recognition of contribution impact
    - Designated spaces for helper emotional processing
    - Structured transitions between helping and receiving
    - Regular assessment of helper wellbeing as community priority

These practical approaches transform abstract values around sustainable helping into concrete systems supporting both individual wellbeing and collective care capacity.

Designing Sustainable Care Systems

Beyond individual approaches and small-group arrangements, apocalyptic times often require deliberately designed care systems that can operate sustainably despite ongoing challenges and limited resources. While comprehensive system design exceeds this chapter's scope, several key principles support creating care structures with lasting resilience.

Core Design Principles from Successful Commons

Researcher Elinor Ostrom (who received the Nobel Prize in Economics for her work studying successful commons management) identified several design principles present in sustainable resource-sharing systems across diverse contexts. These principles, adapted for care systems, include:

1. **Clear boundaries** Well-defined parameters regarding:

   - Who participates and under what conditions
   - What resources and services are shared
   - What responsibilities participation entails
   - How decisions affecting the system are made
   - When and how the system activates for different needs

2. **Proportional benefits and costs** Balanced relationship between contribution and access:

   - Contribution expectations scaled to individual capacity
   - Access rights connected to participation level
   - Recognition of diverse contribution forms
   - Flexible exchange systems accommodating different resources
   - Transparent accounting of both tangible and intangible contributions

3. **Collective choice arrangements** Decision-making processes involving those affected:

   - Accessible participation in rule creation and modification
   - Graduated involvement options at different commitment levels
   - Multiple communication channels for diverse accessibility
   - Transparent decision documentation and distribution
   - Regular review and adjustment based on implementation experience

4. **Monitoring with accountability** Systems ensuring agreement adherence:

    - ○ Multi-level accountability structures
    - ○ Graduated responses to boundary violations
    - ○ Community-based monitoring rather than hierarchical enforcement
    - ○ Restoration-focused rather than punitive approaches
    - ○ Regular system evaluation against stated purposes

5. **Conflict resolution mechanisms** Accessible processes for addressing disagreements:

    - ○ Low-cost initial resolution approaches
    - ○ Graduated options for unresolved conflicts
    - ○ Clear documentation of resolutions creating precedent
    - ○ Cultural norms supporting direct communication
    - ○ Skilled facilitation available for complex situations

6. **Minimal external interference** Protection from outside disruption:

- Recognition of system autonomy by larger institutions
- Formal relationship definition with external entities
- Clear interface protocols with adjacent systems
- Protection of essential functions during external turbulence
- Adaptation capacity for changing external conditions

7. **Nested organization** Multi-level structures appropriate to different functions:

- Small units handling intimate care needs
- Mid-level coordination for resource distribution
- Larger structures for external representation
- Appropriate scale matching for specific functions
- Information flow systems connecting levels

These design principles don't prescribe specific structures but provide guidelines for creating systems adapted to particular contexts while incorporating elements common to sustainable collective arrangements across diverse circumstances.

Resilience-Enhancing System Characteristics

Beyond Ostrom's core principles, several specific characteristics enhance care system resilience during apocalyptic conditions:

1. **Modularity** Organization into relatively independent components that can function autonomously when necessary:

   - Geographic distribution preventing single-point disruption
   - Functional redundancy across system components
   - Independent subsystem operation capability
   - Clear protocols for disconnection and reconnection
   - Information caching at multiple system points
2. **Diversity** Incorporation of varied approaches, resources, and perspectives:

- Multiple skill sets addressing similar needs
- Diverse resource access pathways
- Various communication channels
- Multiple decision-making approaches for different contexts
- Diverse participation modes accommodating different capacities

3. **Feedback responsiveness** Structures enabling rapid adaptation to changing conditions:

- Regular assessment cycles with clear metrics
- Multi-channel feedback gathering
- Explicit adjustment protocols based on outcomes
- Rapid response capacity for urgent modifications
- Learning documentation creating institutional memory

4. **Regenerative design** Systems that replenish rather than merely consume resources:

- Care provider support integrated into core functions
- Skill development incorporated into participation
- Relationship building embedded in practical activities
- Joy and meaning generation alongside task completion
- Resource cultivation alongside resource distribution

5. **Low threshold participation** Accessibility to diverse participants regardless of prior experience:

- Graduated entry points requiring minimal initial commitment
- Clear onboarding processes with explicit guidance
- Skill-building incorporated into participation
- Multiple contribution options matching varied capacities
- Belonging signals independent of contribution quantity

These characteristics create systems capable of withstanding significant disruption while continuing essential care functions—and potentially even growing stronger through adaptive response to challenges.

Implementation Pathways

Moving from design principles to functional systems involves several practical implementation approaches:

1. **Start where you are** Beginning with existing relationships and resources rather than waiting for ideal conditions:

   - Mapping current connections for care potential
   - Identifying immediately available resources
   - Starting with highest-need/highest-capacity intersection
   - Creating simple initial structures with evolution capacity
   - Documenting learning for future expansion

2. **Pilot before scaling** Testing approaches at small scale before wider implementation:

   - Time-limited experimental structures with evaluation

- Clear success metrics defined before implementation
- Documentation supporting knowledge transfer
- Adaptation incorporation before expansion
- Graduated scaling with ongoing adjustment

3. **Template development** Creating reusable frameworks that reduce implementation burden:

- Basic agreements adaptable to specific contexts
- Decision-making processes with clear documentation
- Communication protocols with implementation guides
- Conflict resolution procedures with facilitation guidance
- Resource tracking systems with customization options

4. **Cross-pollination networks** Connections between separate care systems for mutual learning:

- Regular inter-system knowledge exchange
- Comparative outcome assessment
- Complementary experimentation coordination
- Resource sharing for innovation support
- Combined advocacy when appropriate

These implementation approaches acknowledge the reality that perfect systems rarely emerge fully formed but develop through iterative experimentation, evaluation, and adaptation—especially during the complex and changing conditions of apocalyptic times.

When Collective Care Systems Fail

Despite best intentions and careful design, collective care systems sometimes fail, particularly during the extreme challenges of apocalyptic periods. Addressing this reality with clear-eyed pragmatism rather than idealism or despair helps develop appropriate responses when systems don't function as intended.

Common Failure Modes

Several predictable patterns emerge when care systems break down:

1. **Capacity overwhelm** Demand exceeding available resources despite distribution efforts:

    ○ Widespread need exceeding collective capacity
    ○ Simultaneous provider stress reducing response capability
    ○ Rapidly changing conditions outpacing adaptation capacity
    ○ External pressures compromising internal function
    ○ Cascading failures across interconnected systems

2. **Free rider problems** Participation imbalances undermining reciprocity:

    ○ Consistent taking without corresponding contribution
    ○ Invisible care work falling disproportionately on some participants
    ○ Boundary testing without consequence response

- Growing resentment eroding willingness to share
- Gradual system abandonment by consistent contributors

3. **Factional conflict** Disagreements evolving into destructive division:

- Resource allocation disputes without resolution mechanisms
- Value differences manifesting as irreconcilable positions
- Leadership struggles consuming system energy
- External threat response creating internal tension
- Trust breakdown inhibiting cooperation necessary for function

4. **Ossification** Systems becoming rigid and unresponsive:

- Rules supplanting purposes they originally served
- Process complexity creating participation barriers
- Leadership entrenchment preventing necessary evolution

- ○ Disconnection from changing member needs
- ○ Maintenance consuming resources needed for core functions

Recognizing these patterns helps identify system distress before complete failure, potentially enabling intervention while adjustment remains possible.

Response Options for System Failure

When care systems do fail, several response approaches remain available:

1. **Graceful degradation** Strategic function reduction rather than chaotic collapse:

   - ○ Explicit prioritization of essential versus optional services
   - ○ Clear communication about capacity limitations
   - ○ Deliberate release of unsustainable commitments
   - ○ Preservation of core functions at reduced levels
   - ○ Transparent documentation of decision rationale

2. **Component preservation** Maintaining functional elements while acknowledging overall system limitations:

  - Identification of still-working subsystems
  - Protection of vital relationships despite structural breakdown
  - Documentation of effective practices for future reconstruction
  - Resource preservation for eventual rebuilding
  - Continued mini-function where possible despite macro-failure

3. **Intelligent triage** Directing remaining resources based on clear ethical frameworks:

  - Explicit criteria for resource allocation during scarcity
  - Decision processes incorporating diverse perspectives
  - Transparency regarding limitations and rationales
  - Care for those most vulnerable within remaining capacity
  - Balance between immediate needs and longer-term viability

4. **Phoenix planning** Preparing for system rebirth even amid current failure:

   ○ Learning capture from breakdown experience
   ○ Relationship maintenance for future reconstruction
   ○ Resource preservation for rebuilding phases
   ○ Documentation supporting later re-establishment
   ○ Vision maintenance despite temporary implementation inability

These approaches acknowledge system failure without surrendering to complete dissolution of collective care capacity, preserving both practical function where possible and foundational elements necessary for eventual renewal.

Conclusion: The Tapestry of Care

As we conclude this exploration of collective care in collapse, it's worth emphasizing that sustainable approaches rarely involve either purely individual self-care or completely communal systems. Rather, resilience emerges from a tapestry weaving together multiple care levels—personal practices, intimate relationships, small groups, larger networks, and formal structures.

This multi-level tapestry provides redundancy when any single system falters, flexibility adapting to changing circumstances, and appropriate scale matching for different needs. Self-care practices preserve individual capacity for contribution; dyadic relationships provide intimate support; small groups manage practical care tasks; wider networks distribute larger resource loads; and formal structures interface with existing institutions.

During apocalyptic times, this tapestry often develops holes—places where particular threads or sections unravel due to disruption, depletion, or system failure. Perfect, comprehensive care coverage becomes unrealistic. Yet the tapestry metaphor reminds us that repair remains possible, that function continues even with some damage, and that patterns of care persist even when individual threads break.

The practices explored in this chapter—from capacity-based contribution to micro-network development to sustainable system design— provide tools for both maintaining and repairing this essential tapestry of care during periods when it faces its greatest challenges.

Perhaps most importantly, the tapestry metaphor reminds us that care has always been collective— that the myth of purely individual self-sufficiency obscures the interdependent reality of human survival and flourishing throughout our existence. Apocalyptic conditions don't create this interdependence but reveal it by stripping away the systems that previously obscured it.

In the next chapter, we'll explore another essential dimension of navigating apocalyptic times: finding and maintaining hope without delusion— developing relationship to possible futures that neither denies difficult realities nor surrenders to despair about what might yet emerge.

CHAPTER 14: Hope Without Delusion

"How can I possibly have hope when everything seems to be getting worse?"

This question haunts many people navigating apocalyptic times—perhaps including you. It's a question that emerges from the painful gap between our desires for a better world and the seemingly relentless progression of crises we witness daily. Climate disruption accelerates. Democracy falters. Inequality deepens. Violence continues. Systems we rely on increasingly fail to serve basic human needs.

In the face of these realities, conventional hope often feels naïve at best, delusional at worst. The sunny optimism that "everything will work out fine" collides with mounting evidence suggesting otherwise. Yet surrender to complete hopelessness creates its own problems—psychological despair that undermines wellbeing, and political passivity that abandons the possibility of positive influence.

This chapter explores a third path: hope without delusion. Not the blind optimism that denies difficulty, nor the fatalistic despair that forecloses possibility, but a clear-eyed hope that acknowledges harsh realities while maintaining genuine openness to positive emergence. This paradoxical position—simultaneously holding awareness of what's being lost and commitment to what might yet be created—offers both psychological sustenance and political efficacy during apocalyptic times.

The Case for Cautious Optimism

Before exploring specific approaches to hope without delusion, let's examine the evidence-based case for cautious optimism even during apocalyptic times. This isn't about cherry-picking positive news to counterbalance negative events, but understanding deeper patterns that justify continued hope despite undeniable challenges.

Historical Precedent for Emergence

Throughout human history, periods of severe disruption have sometimes—not always, but sometimes—generated significant positive developments that would have seemed impossible before the crisis. Several patterns suggest potential for similar emergence during current apocalyptic conditions:

1. **Crisis-catalyzed innovation** Historical examples abound of accelerated innovation during periods when existing systems failed to address emerging challenges:
   - The Black Death's devastation eventually contributed to labor system transformations that improved conditions for surviving workers
   - The Great Depression ultimately generated new economic models and social safety nets
   - World War II's resource constraints produced technological advances that later supported widespread prosperity
   - The AIDS crisis catalyzed transformations in both medical

research approaches and LGBTQ+
community organization

These examples don't minimize the suffering these
crises caused but illustrate how system breakdown
sometimes accelerates innovation in ways stability
rarely does.

2. **Value clarification through loss** Collapsing
   systems often reveal previously obscured
   values, creating clearer consensus around
   priorities:
   - Public health crises highlight the
     importance of previously undervalued
     care work
   - Environmental disasters demonstrate
     the fundamental value of healthy
     ecosystems
   - Political breakdowns clarify the
     essential nature of civic norms and
     institutions
   - Economic crashes reveal the
     importance of economic security and
     material sufficiency

This value clarification, while often emerging
through painful loss, sometimes generates social
consensus that enables more aligned
reconstruction efforts.

3. **Latent capacity activation** Crisis frequently reveals human capabilities that remained dormant during periods of relative stability:
    - Disaster research consistently shows widespread prosocial behavior emerging during acute crises
    - Historical records document remarkable community self-organization during system breakdown
    - Biographical accounts reveal unexpected personal growth catalyzed by navigating collapse
    - Case studies show accelerated social innovation during periods when conventional approaches fail

These capacity activations suggest humans possess greater adaptive potential than normally expressed during stable periods—potential that becomes accessible precisely when most needed.

None of these patterns guarantee positive outcomes from current apocalyptic conditions. History also contains examples of crises leading to further deterioration rather than regenerative response. However, they provide evidence-based grounds for maintaining openness to possible positive emergence alongside clear recognition of present difficulties.

The Multiplicity of Parallel Trends

Another basis for cautious optimism involves recognizing that apocalyptic times rarely contain solely negative developments. Most periods feature multiple contradictory trends operating simultaneously:

1. **Simultaneous destruction and creation**
   Nearly all historical periods reveal concurrent processes of both breakdown and emergence:
   - While certain industries collapse, others develop in response to changing conditions
   - As some cultural forms disappear, new expressions emerge from changed circumstances
   - When certain relationship patterns become untenable, alternative forms develop
   - While some knowledge becomes obsolete, new understanding emerges

These parallel processes mean even during significant collapse, seeds of new possibilities simultaneously develop.

2. **Different trajectories at different scales**
   Assessment of whether conditions are

"improving" or "deteriorating" often depends on which scale receives primary attention:

- ○ Global trends may differ significantly from local developments
- ○ Long-term trajectories often contradict short-term fluctuations
- ○ Macro-system patterns may oppose micro-system evolutions
- ○ Different sectors or domains may follow opposing trajectories simultaneously

This multi-scale complexity means narratives of universal deterioration rarely capture the full picture of apocalyptic periods.

3. **Pendulum dynamics in social systems**
   Many social patterns follow pendulum-like swings rather than linear trajectories:
   - ○ Periods of increasing authoritarianism often generate subsequent democracy movements
   - ○ Economic inequality tends to produce eventual correction through policy or disruption
   - ○ Cultural homogenization frequently catalyzes diversity renaissance
   - ○ Materialistic excess regularly generates spiritual/relational renewal

These oscillating patterns suggest even negative trends may contain seeds of their own reversal rather than continuing indefinitely.

Again, these observations don't justify complacent optimism about current challenges. Pendulums sometimes break rather than swing back; scales can collapse rather than merely shift; creation doesn't always compensate for simultaneous destruction. However, they provide reasonable grounds for remaining open to positive possibilities alongside clear awareness of difficult realities.

The Limited Predictability Horizon

Perhaps the strongest case for cautious optimism involves the inherent limitations of prediction during complex system reorganization. Numerous fields— from meteorology to economics to ecology— demonstrate that prediction reliability decreases exponentially as time horizons extend, particularly during periods of system transformation.

Several factors create this prediction limitation:

1. **Non-linear causality** Small inputs sometimes generate disproportionately large effects through feedback loops, making long-term outcomes highly sensitive to minor variations impossible to forecast accurately.

2. **Emergent properties** Complex systems regularly develop properties unpredictable from component analysis, as interactions between elements create capacities absent in individual parts.

3. **Novel condition response** Past behavior patterns provide decreasing predictive value during unprecedented conditions, as systems develop new responses to novel circumstances.

4. **Human agency complexity** Collective human response involves consciousness, meaning-making, and innovation capacities that introduce fundamental unpredictability into social system trajectories.

These limitations mean confident predictions of inevitably catastrophic futures represent epistemic overreach rather than evidence-based assessment. While apocalyptic outcomes constitute genuine possibilities deserving serious consideration, they represent probabilities rather than certainties—leaving legitimate space for other possibilities including unexpectedly positive developments.

This limited predictability horizon provides perhaps the most solid foundation for hope without delusion: not certainty that desired outcomes will manifest, but genuine uncertainty that legitimately includes both negative and positive possibilities.

Finding Meaning Without Requiring Happy Endings

While the previous section establishes reasonable grounds for cautious optimism, genuine hope without delusion requires deeper foundations than mere possibility of positive outcomes. It requires frameworks for finding meaning regardless of how circumstances ultimately unfold—approaches that neither depend on guaranteed happy endings nor surrender to nihilistic meaninglessness when preferred outcomes appear increasingly unlikely.

Transforming Hope from Expectation to Practice

One key shift involves reconceptualizing hope itself —moving from passive expectation about future outcomes to active practice in present engagement.

Several perspectives support this transformation:

1. **Hope as orientation rather than prediction**
   Understanding hope as a way of relating to possibility rather than specific outcome expectation:

   - Maintaining openness to positive emergence without requiring certainty
   - Continuing constructive action despite outcome uncertainty
   - Cultivating receptivity to unexpected positive developments
   - Preserving imaginative capacity for alternative futures
   - Resisting premature closure of possibility despite discouraging evidence

2. **Hope as discipline rather than feeling**
   Approaching hope as intentional practice maintained through commitment rather than emotional state dependent on external conditions:

- ○ Regular cultivation regardless of circumstantial fluctuation
- ○ Deliberate choice renewed daily rather than automatic response
- ○ Community-supported practice rather than isolated individual state
- ○ Skillful capacity developed through practice rather than intrinsic trait
- ○ Tradition-embedded approach with historical continuity

3. **Hope as witness rather than prediction**
Framing hope as bearing witness to present generative possibilities rather than projecting guaranteed future manifestations:

- ○ Attention to currently active positive developments regardless of scale
- ○ Recognition of human capacity demonstrations in present circumstances
- ○ Acknowledgment of justice work already underway despite opposition
- ○ Appreciation of beauty and meaning created amid difficulty
- ○ Witness to resilience and creativity in current responses

These perspectives transform hope from dependency on particular outcomes to sustainable practice possible regardless of external circumstances—not through denial of reality but through different relationship to both present conditions and future possibilities.

Meaning Frameworks Beyond Progress Narratives

Another key shift involves developing meaning frameworks that don't depend on conventional progress narratives increasingly contradicted by apocalyptic experiences. Several alternative meaning approaches offer sustenance without requiring ever-improving conditions:

1. **Cyclical rather than linear time**
   Understanding history through cycles of growth, decline, release, and renewal rather than continuous advancement:

   - Natural cycle integration (seasons, lifespans, ecological succession)
   - Recognition of civilizational patterns across rise and decline
   - Value in all cycle phases rather than only growth periods

- Connection to ancestors who navigated similar cycle points
- Orientation toward future cycle emergence beyond current decline

2. **Contribution rather than outcome orientation** Finding meaning in one's contribution regardless of ultimate results:

- Value in bearing witness independent of prevention capacity
- Worth in alleviating suffering even without eliminating its causes
- Meaning through right relationship to challenges regardless of resolution
- Significance in expressing core values through action despite outcomes
- Purpose through participating in shared effort beyond individual impact

3. **Intrinsic rather than instrumental valuation** Recognizing inherent worth independent of future utility or continuation:

- Beauty appreciation regardless of permanence
- Relationship value independent of duration

- Experience meaning not requiring continuation
- Present flourishing significance separate from future prospects
- Inherent worth recognition regardless of instrumental outcomes

4. **Faithful presence amid uncertainty** Finding meaning in showing up fully despite outcome ambiguity:

- Integrity through alignment with values regardless of effectiveness
- Purpose through conscious choice amid limitation
- Meaning via faithfulness to commitments despite unclear results
- Value in embodying alternatives regardless of their ultimate prevalence
- Significance through quality of presence rather than quantity of impact

These frameworks don't eliminate desire for positive outcomes but create meaning foundations that remain stable regardless of whether preferred futures materialize—sustaining both psychological wellbeing and capacity for continued engagement during periods when conventional progress narratives increasingly fail to match lived experience.

Tragedy as Meaning Source

Perhaps most counterintuitively, genuine hope without delusion often incorporates rather than avoids tragedy as potential meaning source. Throughout human experience, some of our most profound meaning has emerged not from unmitigated success but from engagement with genuine loss, limitation, and difficulty.

Several traditions illuminate this paradoxical relationship between tragedy and meaning:

1. **The aesthetic tradition** Throughout human cultural history, tragedy as art form has generated deep meaning precisely through confronting rather than avoiding difficult realities:
   - Greek tragedy's exploration of human limitation and contradiction
   - Shakespeare's engagement with inescapable human flaws
   - Modern literature's unflinching witness to genuine suffering
   - Indigenous storytelling incorporating loss alongside resilience

- ○ Religious narratives integrating sacrifice and redemption

These traditions suggest meaning often emerges not despite tragedy but through honest engagement with it.

2. **The existentialist perspective** Philosophical existentialism proposes that facing rather than denying life's inherent difficulties creates authentic rather than illusory meaning:
   - ○ Confronting mortality as catalyst for genuine living
   - ○ Acknowledging absurdity while choosing meaningful engagement
   - ○ Accepting responsibility amid limitation
   - ○ Creating purpose through choice rather than discovery
   - ○ Finding freedom within rather than from constraint

This tradition suggests honest recognition of difficulty enables rather than prevents authentic meaning creation.

3. **The depth psychology approach** Various psychological traditions propose that integrating rather than avoiding shadow aspects of experience generates wholeness rather than fragmentation:

- Jung's individuation through shadow integration
- Frankl's meaning creation amid extreme suffering
- Contemporary trauma research on post-traumatic growth
- Transpersonal psychology's darkness engagement for wholeness
- Narrative therapy's complexity incorporation for coherence

These approaches suggest psychological wholeness requires incorporating rather than bypassing difficult dimensions of experience.

4. **The religious wisdom dimension** Diverse spiritual traditions include engagement with suffering as essential rather than peripheral to meaning discovery:
   - Christianity's crucifixion-resurrection relationship
   - Buddhism's suffering acknowledgment in Four Noble Truths
   - Judaism's exile-return dynamics
   - Indigenous traditions incorporating loss within ceremony
   - Mystical approaches across traditions embracing dark night experiences

These traditions suggest spiritual depth often emerges through rather than despite confrontation with genuine tragedy.

Incorporating these perspectives doesn't romanticize suffering or surrender to fatalism. Rather, it creates meaning possibilities that neither require denying apocalyptic realities nor collapse under their weight—finding depth precisely through honest engagement with difficulty alongside continued openness to unexpected grace.

Planting Trees Under Whose Shade You'll Never Sit

Beyond psychological meaning frameworks, hope without delusion involves practical approaches to action amid uncertainty. One particularly powerful metaphor involves "planting trees under whose shade you'll never sit"—taking meaningful action whose full benefits may emerge beyond your lifetime or direct experience.

This approach transforms the relationship between action and outcome in several significant ways:

Intergenerational Timeframes

Hope without delusion often involves extending timeframes beyond individual lifespans to intergenerational perspectives. This shift creates several possibilities unavailable within conventional short-term frameworks:

1. **Legacy thinking** Considering impacts extending beyond personal experience:

   - Asking "what am I leaving for those who come after?"
   - Evaluating actions based on multi-generational effects
   - Creating resources with long-term rather than immediate utility
   - Developing capacities with extended rather than immediate application
   - Preserving options for future generations despite uncertain specifics

2. **Historical contextualization** Placing current efforts within longer historical arcs:

   - Recognizing precedents for delayed manifestation of justice efforts
   - Studying historical examples of seemingly futile actions later proving crucial

- Identifying patterns of apparent regression preceding significant advance
- Learning from ancestors who worked toward futures they never saw completed
- Drawing sustenance from movements spanning multiple generations

3. **Slow hope cultivation** Developing capacity for hope operating on longer timescales than immediate gratification:

- Practices appreciating subtle, gradual positive developments
- Regular attention to slow-moving but significant trends
- Celebration of small shifts with long-term implications
- Acknowledgment of foundation-building preceding visible change
- Recognition of preparation creating possibility for later manifestation

These approaches don't eliminate desire for immediate positive change but create capacity for meaningful action regardless of whether benefits manifest within personally experienced timeframes.

Uncertain Outcome Engagement

Beyond timeframe extension, this approach involves developing capacity for committed action despite outcome uncertainty. Several practices support this challenging orientation:

1. **Non-attachment action** Engagement combining full commitment with open-handed relationship to results:

   - Acting with complete presence while releasing outcome fixation
   - Bringing best effort without identifying self-worth with results
   - Evaluating actions by alignment with values rather than external success
   - Maintaining flexibility as circumstances change without abandoning purpose
   - Finding satisfaction in process quality regardless of outcome manifestation

2. **Possibility rather than probability orientation** Focusing on what might be possible rather than what seems most probable:

   - Asking "what possibilities exist?" rather than just "what's most likely?"

- Taking action creating potential for positive outcomes even when uncertain
- Maintaining alertness to unexpected openings amid discouraging conditions
- Developing capacity to act on possibility without requiring certainty
- Creating conditions that increase desirable outcome possibility without guarantees

3. **Present integrity focus** Grounding action in present integrity rather than future results:

- Asking "what does faithfulness require now?" rather than "will this succeed?"
- Finding meaning in alignment between values and actions regardless of outcomes
- Creating present manifestations of desired futures regardless of their durability
- Focusing on what remains within influence rather than lamenting what doesn't
- Measuring success by response quality rather than external results

These approaches transform hope from dependency on particular outcomes to capacity for meaningful engagement regardless of whether preferred results ultimately manifest.

Seed-Scattering Rather Than Monument-Building

Metaphorically, this orientation often involves shift from monument-building to seed-scattering—from creating single massive achievements to distributing many small possibilities, some of which may flourish in unexpected conditions.

This approach manifests through several practical strategies:

1. **Diverse simultaneous initiatives**
   Developing multiple parallel efforts rather than singular focus:

   - Distributing energy across various promising directions
   - Maintaining various approaches addressing similar challenges
   - Supporting multiple solution pathways rather than selecting one "best" approach
   - Creating portfolio of initiatives with different timescales and probabilities

- Ensuring some continuation regardless of which specific approaches succeed

2. **Resilience through redundancy** Building overlapping systems rather than maximizing efficiency:

   - Creating backup approaches for core functions
   - Developing alternatives before primary systems fail
   - Maintaining seemingly redundant capacities for adaptation potential
   - Preserving diverse options for uncertain future conditions
   - Prioritizing system persistence over performance optimization

3. **Option creation rather than path certainty** Focusing on increasing available options rather than committing to specific trajectories:

   - Preserving freedom of action in uncertain futures
   - Creating resources usable in various potential scenarios
   - Developing capacities applicable across multiple possible conditions

- ○ Maintaining flexible response potential rather than rigid plans
- ○ Prioritizing adaptation capacity over prediction accuracy

These approaches transform relationship to uncertain futures from attempting to ensure specific outcomes to creating conditions where positive possibilities remain viable regardless of which specific developments ultimately manifest.

Navigating Between Premature Hope and Premature Despair

While the preceding sections address hope's foundations and practical manifestations, effective navigation of apocalyptic times also requires discernment between appropriate and premature versions of both hope and despair. Neither naive optimism nor fatalistic pessimism serves well during complex system transition; skilled discernment regarding when to maintain hope versus when to acknowledge likely loss becomes essential.

Recognizing Premature Hope

Several indicators suggest hope may be premature or misplaced regarding specific situations:

1. **Evidence dismissal patterns** Consistently ignoring or minimizing data contradicting preferred narratives:

   - Selective attention to positive while dismissing negative indicators
   - Requiring higher evidence standards for unwelcome than welcome information
   - Attributing confirming data to pattern while dismissing contradicting data as anomaly
   - Constructing elaborate explanations to preserve optimism despite contrary evidence
   - Attacking messengers rather than engaging messages when information threatens hope

2. **Fixed timeline attachment** Maintaining specific outcome expectations despite repeated timeline failures:

   - Moving prediction goalposts without acknowledging previous inaccuracy
   - Continuing belief in imminent breakthrough despite multiple delays

- Attributing timing failures to circumstantial rather than fundamental factors
- Ignoring accumulating evidence of systematic rather than temporary obstacles
- Dismissing pattern recognition suggesting fundamental rather than incidental barriers

3. **Psychological function primacy** Prioritizing hope's comfort function over its guidance function:

- Resisting information that would require difficult adjustment
- Maintaining narratives primarily because alternatives feel intolerable
- Dismissing perspectives that would necessitate painful acceptance
- Prioritizing emotional comfort over response effectiveness
- Avoiding reconsideration despite accumulating contradictory evidence

These patterns suggest hope functioning as denial mechanism rather than authentic engagement with both difficulty and possibility—likely requiring adjustment toward greater reality acknowledgment for genuine rather than delusional hope.

Recognizing Premature Despair

Conversely, several indicators suggest despair may be premature regarding other situations:

1. **Certainty beyond evidence** Expressing greater certainty about negative outcomes than available data justifies:

    - Claiming inevitable collapse despite complex system unpredictability
    - Asserting comprehensive understanding of highly complex dynamics
    - Dismissing adaptation possibilities despite historical precedent
    - Ignoring emergent responses already developing
    - Overlooking limitations in prediction capacity during system transition
2. **Terminal diagnosis errors** Mistaking serious difficulties for terminal conditions:

    - Conflating significant challenges with insurmountable obstacles

- ○ Failing to distinguish between decline and complete collapse
- ○ Assuming current trajectory continues without intervention possibility
- ○ Overlooking historical examples of apparent terminal conditions overcome
- ○ Discounting human innovation capacity under extreme pressure

3. **Protective despair dynamics** Using despair as psychological protection against disappointment:

- ○ Preemptive hopelessness to avoid potential disappointment
- ○ Using certainty of failure to justify disengagement
- ○ Cultivating cynicism as sophistication marker
- ○ Adopting pessimism as risk management strategy
- ○ Employing despair as retroactive justification for inaction

These patterns suggest despair functioning as premature foreclosure rather than legitimate acknowledgment of genuine limitation—likely requiring adjustment toward greater possibility recognition for appropriate discernment.

Developing Discernment Capacity

Beyond recognizing potential hope or despair distortions, developing fundamental discernment capacity helps navigate between premature versions of either orientation. Several practices support this essential skill:

1. **Epistemic humility cultivation** Developing appropriate relationship to knowledge limitations:

   - Regular acknowledgment of prediction constraints
   - Comfort with provisional rather than absolute conclusions
   - Explicit uncertainty incorporation in assessment
   - Awareness of one's own biases and emotional influences
   - Recognition of complexity exceeding comprehensive understanding

2. **Holding space practices** Maintaining capacity to hold contradictory information simultaneously:

   - Both/and rather than either/or thinking development

- ○ Paradox tolerance without premature resolution
- ○ Remaining in productive tension between known and unknown
- ○ Developing capacity for nuance without collapsing to false clarity
- ○ Comfort with provisional meanings subject to revision

3. **Diverse perspective integration**
Deliberately incorporating viewpoints challenging preferred narratives:

- ○ Seeking input from those with different assessments
- ○ Engaging strongest versions of opposing perspectives
- ○ Identifying partial truth in contradictory viewpoints
- ○ Developing regular practices exposing position limitations
- ○ Creating discussion contexts where perspective diversity receives welcome

4. **Regular reconsideration practices**
Establishing structures for ongoing assessment adjustment:

- Scheduled evaluation of previous expectations against outcomes
- Decision documentation enabling later accuracy assessment
- Explicit threshold identification triggering position reconsideration
- Prediction journaling with regular review
- Community discernment rather than isolated judgment

These practices develop capacity for appropriate discernment between situations where hope remains justified versus those where acceptance of likely loss better serves both psychological wellbeing and effective response.

Hope as Climate Rather Than Weather

A final framework for hope without delusion involves distinguishing between hope as climate versus weather—between fundamental orientation maintained through fluctuation versus dependent on specific momentary conditions.

The Distinction Between Climate and Weather

In meteorological terms, weather describes specific atmospheric conditions at particular moments, while climate describes long-term patterns that persist despite daily fluctuation. Similarly, hope as climate describes fundamental orientation toward possibility that persists through circumstantial variation, while hope as weather depends on specific encouraging developments.

Several characteristics distinguish climate-hope from weather-hope:

1. **Persistence through fluctuation** Climate-hope maintains fundamental orientation despite temporary setbacks:

    ◦ Continuing engagement through disappointing developments
    ◦ Maintaining possibility orientation during discouraging periods
    ◦ Returning to fundamental commitment after temporary discouragement
    ◦ Distinguishing between momentary feelings and core orientation
    ◦ Rebound capacity after inevitable disappointments

2. **Foundation beyond circumstance** Climate-hope grounds itself in deeper foundations

than external conditions:

- Values-based rather than results-based commitment
- Identity connection beyond strategic calculation
- Community-embedded rather than isolated individual stance
- Historical continuity transcending present circumstances
- Tradition connection providing multi-generational context

3. **Integration of difficulty** Climate-hope incorporates rather than requires absence of challenge:

- Accommodation of genuine loss without orientation abandonment
- Capacity to honor grief while maintaining possibility orientation
- Integration of disappointment without fundamental surrender
- Acceptance of partial failure without total disengagement
- Relationship to limitation that neither denies nor capitulates

These distinctions transform hope from fragile dependency on favorable conditions to resilient capacity maintained even during inevitable difficulties—not through denial but through deeper foundations capable of weathering storms while maintaining fundamental orientation.

Practices Supporting Climate-Hope

Several specific practices help develop and maintain climate-hope capacity:

1. **Anchor experiences** Identifying and regularly reconnecting with foundational hope sources:

    - Powerful memories demonstrating possibility
    - Relationship connections providing ongoing inspiration
    - Physical locations embedding hope experience
    - Texts, images, or music carrying hope reminders
    - Practices reliably generating recommitment

2. **Seasonal frameworks** Developing approaches acknowledging inevitable mood and perception fluctuation:

- Preparation during hopeful periods for subsequent difficult phases
- External support structures compensating during low-hope periods
- Acceptance of natural oscillation without questioning core orientation
- Community practices sustaining individuals during personal troughs
- Ritual acknowledgment of seasonal patterns in hope experience

3. **Tradition connection** Linking personal hope orientation to larger historical continuities:

- Stories connecting current challenges to previous generations
- Practices maintaining connection across time to ancestors facing difficulty
- Identification with movements spanning multiple generations
- Role models demonstrating lifetime commitment through fluctuation
- Legacy perspectives extending beyond individual experience

4. **Transcendent grounding** Connecting hope to sources beyond immediate circumstances:

- Spiritual traditions offering meaning frameworks transcending conditions
- Philosophical approaches providing foundation beyond preference
- Aesthetic experiences generating hope undeducible from facts alone
- Natural cycles demonstrating renewal beyond apparent endings
- Mystery engagement beyond comprehensive rational understanding

These practices cultivate hope as fundamental climate sustained through inevitable weather variations rather than dependent on consistent favorable conditions—creating resilience during apocalyptic times when encouraging developments may prove inconsistent at best.

CHAPTER 15: The Joy of Being Alive Anyway

We've traveled a long road together through this book—exploring everything from grief and humor to practical skills and collective care to hope without delusion. Now, in this final chapter, we arrive at perhaps the most fundamental question of all: How do we find joy in being alive anyway, despite all the reasons not to be?

This isn't about toxic positivity or forced happiness. It's about the genuine, sometimes surprising joy that emerges not despite difficult realities but somehow alongside them—the strange miracle of finding yourself laughing during grief, experiencing moments of transcendent connection amid collapse, or feeling inexplicably alive precisely when you'd expect to feel most defeated.

These experiences aren't anomalies or distractions from reality. They represent a profound truth about human existence: that beauty, meaning, and joy remain possible even in the darkest circumstances. Not as compensation that somehow "makes up for" suffering, but as parallel dimensions of experience that exist simultaneously with difficulty.

In this chapter, we'll explore approaches to embracing this complex totality—not to bypass the hard parts but to experience life in its full, messy, contradictory wholeness. We'll examine practices that help create space for joy without denial, connection without escape, and aliveness without pretending everything is fine when it clearly isn't.

Embracing the Messy Middle

One of the most challenging aspects of apocalyptic times involves what might be called "the messy middle"—the reality that most situations aren't either completely terrible or absolutely wonderful but complex mixtures of beauty and brokenness, hope and grief, connection and loss.

The Binary Thinking Trap

Human cognition naturally gravitates toward binary thinking—categorizing experiences as good or bad, success or failure, reason for hope or cause for despair. During particularly challenging times, this tendency often intensifies as our threat-detection systems heighten, pushing us toward black-and-white assessments that might have served survival functions in our evolutionary past but limit our capacity to engage with complex present realities.

This binary thinking creates several significant problems:

1. **Reality distortion** Binary frameworks inevitably oversimplify complex situations, forcing multifaceted experiences into reductive categories that distort rather than clarify.

2. **Experience constriction** When we automatically categorize entire situations as "bad," we often miss embedded moments of beauty, connection, or meaning that exist within otherwise challenging circumstances.

3. **Response limitation** Binary thinking restricts our response repertoire, pulling us toward

either full engagement with situations deemed "good" or complete withdrawal from those labeled "bad," rather than nuanced, partial, or ambivalent responses.

4. **Emotional overwhelm** When entire complex situations receive negative categorization, the emotional impact often becomes overwhelming rather than manageable, leading to shutdown rather than skillful navigation.

During apocalyptic times, these binary thinking patterns often manifest as pressure to adopt either unrealistic optimism that denies genuine problems or comprehensive pessimism that dismisses real possibilities—with both approaches preventing authentic engagement with the messy middle where most of life actually unfolds.

The Both/And Alternative

Moving beyond binary thinking involves developing capacity for both/and rather than either/or orientation—recognizing that seemingly contradictory experiences often coexist rather than exclude each other:

1. **Simultaneous truths** Acknowledging multiple truths that exist concurrently despite apparent contradiction:

    - Systems are collapsing AND new possibilities are emerging
    - Tremendous suffering exists AND remarkable beauty remains accessible
    - Grievous losses accumulate AND unexpected gifts appear
    - Serious threats intensify AND genuine progress occurs in some areas
    - Personal limits constrain action AND meaningful contribution remains possible

2. **Emotional complexity** Developing capacity to experience seemingly contradictory emotions without requiring resolution:

    - Grief AND gratitude
    - Anger AND tenderness
    - Anxiety AND curiosity
    - Disappointment AND wonder
    - Weariness AND enthusiasm

3. **Partial engagement** Creating approaches that permit engagement with situations despite significant problems:

- Appreciating what works while acknowledging what doesn't
- Contributing where possible while accepting what can't be changed
- Enjoying available pleasures without requiring absence of difficulty
- Creating beauty alongside efforts addressing destruction
- Finding meaning within rather than beyond limitation

These both/and approaches don't resolve the tensions inherent in apocalyptic times but create space to experience their full complexity rather than collapsing to simplified narratives that inevitably exclude important dimensions of reality.

Practices for Messy Middle Navigation

Several specific practices help develop capacity for navigating this messy middle:

1. **Cognitive reframing** Deliberately shifting from binary to complex interpretation frameworks:

- Replacing "either/or" with "both/and" language
- Questioning automatic categorical assessments
- Practicing perspective multiplicity rather than singularity
- Developing comfort with seemingly contradictory viewpoints
- Seeking nuance rather than certainty

2. **Complexity journaling** Regular documentation of experience complexity rather than reductive summaries:

- Recording seemingly contradictory aspects of significant experiences
- Noting unexpected positive elements within difficulties
- Documenting challenging dimensions within generally positive situations
- Tracking emotional complexity rather than dominant feelings alone
- Practicing non-resolution of apparent contradictions

3. **Mixed-experience conversation** Dialogue practices that incorporate rather than resolve complexity:

- Creating conversation spaces welcoming multiple perspectives
- Practicing "yes, and" rather than "yes, but" responses
- Developing language for partial agreement/disagreement
- Exploring seemingly contradictory viewpoints with curiosity
- Resisting pressure toward premature consensus

4. **Paradox meditation** Contemplative practices specifically engaging apparent contradictions:

- Holding opposing concepts simultaneously in awareness
- Breathing into rather than attempting to resolve tension
- Noticing resistance to contradiction without acting on it
- Exploring phenomenological experience of paradox
- Developing comfort with ambiguity through deliberate practice

These practices gradually expand capacity for engaging the messy middle where joy and sorrow, beauty and destruction, hope and grief intertwine rather than separate—creating space for the joy of being alive anyway without requiring denial of difficulty.

The Perfectly Imperfect Art of Catastrophe Living

Beyond embracing complexity, finding joy amid apocalyptic times involves developing what might be called "catastrophe aesthetics"—the capacity to find beauty not despite but sometimes within imperfection, brokenness, and limitation.

From Perfection to Wabi-Sabi

Many cultures, particularly Western industrial ones, emphasize ideals of perfection, completion, and flawlessness—whether in products, experiences, or even personal development. These frameworks often leave little room for finding beauty or satisfaction amid obvious imperfection, breakdown, or limitation.

Alternative aesthetic traditions offer different possibilities. The Japanese concept of wabi-sabi provides one particularly relevant example—finding beauty specifically in impermanence, incompleteness, and imperfection rather than despite them. This perspective derives aesthetic appreciation from:

1. **Impermanence markers** Finding beauty in signs of transience rather than permanence:

    ◦ Weathering and patina rather than newness
    ◦ Seasonal changes rather than unchanging stability
    ◦ Evolutionary processes rather than fixed forms
    ◦ Cycles of growth and decay rather than stasis
    ◦ Ephemerality rather than durability
2. **Irregularity appreciation** Valuing unique irregularities rather than standardized perfection:

    ◦ Natural variation rather than mechanical uniformity
    ◦ Organic asymmetry rather than geometric precision
    ◦ Unexpected emergence rather than complete control
    ◦ Unique particularity rather than generic perfection
    ◦ Character-giving flaws rather than flawlessness

3. **Incompletion openness** Finding beauty in unfinished or partial elements rather than only in completion:

   - Process rather than only final product
   - Potential rather than only actualization
   - Becoming rather than only being
   - Questions rather than only answers
   - Beginnings and middles rather than only endings

This wabi-sabi perspective doesn't romanticize suffering or pretend breakdown is desirable. Rather, it expands aesthetic appreciation beyond conventional perfection to include dimensions of experience often excluded from narrower frameworks—dimensions particularly relevant during times when conventional ideals become increasingly inaccessible.

The Aesthetics of Repair

Beyond appreciating imperfection, finding joy amid apocalyptic conditions often involves cultivating specific aesthetics of repair—finding beauty not just in brokenness itself but in the processes of mending, healing, and reconstituting what's been damaged.

Several traditions offer relevant wisdom:

1. **Kintsugi practice** The Japanese art of repairing broken pottery with gold-infused lacquer, creating objects more beautiful after breakage than before—not by hiding damage but by transforming it into a central aesthetic element.

2. **Visible mending movements** Contemporary approaches to clothing repair that deliberately highlight rather than conceal patches, darning, and other mending techniques— celebrating repair history as integral to an item's beauty and value.

3. **Ecological succession appreciation** Finding beauty in how natural systems heal after disturbance—the particular aesthetics of meadows reclaiming abandoned lots, pioneering species colonizing fire-scarred landscapes, or forests slowly regenerating after storms.

4. **Adaptive reuse architecture** Architectural approaches incorporating rather than erasing

a structure's previous iterations—preserving visible layers of history while adding new elements that engage with rather than conceal past uses.

5. **Musical traditions incorporating breakdown** From blues to kintsugi soundscapes, musical forms that deliberately incorporate dissonance, noise, and unconventional sounds typically considered "mistakes" within conventional frameworks.

These repair aesthetics create possibilities for finding beauty specifically in how we respond to damage and disruption rather than requiring either pristine preservation or complete replacement—possibilities particularly valuable during apocalyptic times when both prevention and comprehensive renewal often exceed available capacity.

Practices for Catastrophe Aesthetics

Several specific practices help develop capacity for finding beauty amid obvious imperfection and breakdown:

1. **Intentional attention** Deliberately directing attention toward elements typically overlooked by conventional aesthetic frameworks:

   - Spending time with weathered rather than new objects
   - Seeking beauty in adaptation rather than original design
   - Observing ecological succession in disturbed areas
   - Noticing emergent order within apparent disorder
   - Appreciating visible history in repaired objects

2. **Documentation practices** Creating records of beauty found within rather than despite difficulty:

   - Photographing unexpected beauty in damaged landscapes
   - Recording stories embedding joy within challenge narratives
   - Collecting examples of repair more beautiful than original
   - Journaling about complexity incorporating both struggle and grace

- Creating art engaging rather than avoiding imperfection

3. **Language expansion** Developing vocabulary beyond binary beautiful/ugly categorization:

   - Learning aesthetic terminology from traditions embracing imperfection
   - Creating personal language for complex aesthetic experiences
   - Practicing nuanced description of mixed aesthetic elements
   - Exploring poetry specifically engaging beauty-within-brokenness
   - Reading literature from traditions with developed imperfection aesthetics

4. **Creation incorporating limitation** Making things that work with rather than against available constraints:

   - Creating art using materials at hand rather than ideal supplies
   - Cooking beautiful meals with limited available ingredients
   - Designing within rather than attempting to transcend restrictions

- ○ Incorporating repurposed elements rather than only new components
- ○ Finding beauty in adaptation to limitation rather than its absence

These practices gradually develop capacity to find genuine aesthetic pleasure within conditions that conventional frameworks might categorize as irredeemably ugly, broken, or failed—not through lowered standards but through expanded aesthetic appreciation particularly suited to apocalyptic times.

Why Showing Up Matters, Even in Apocalypse Pajamas

Beyond embracing complexity and finding beauty amid imperfection, joy during apocalyptic times often emerges through continued participation—showing up for life even when doing so imperfectly, partially, or while wearing metaphorical (or literal) apocalypse pajamas.

The Participation Paradox

One of the great paradoxes of human experience involves the relationship between participation and joy. While we often delay engagement until we feel sufficiently prepared, enthusiastic, or "ready," research consistently shows that participation itself frequently generates these states rather than requiring them as prerequisites.

Several mechanisms create this paradoxical relationship:

1. **State following action** Psychological research demonstrates emotional states often follow rather than precede behavior—with actions like smiling, moving vigorously, or engaging socially triggering corresponding emotional responses regardless of initial feelings.

2. **Activation thresholds** Starting engagement usually requires more energy than continuing it—with activation thresholds protecting us from constant activity but sometimes preventing experiences that would prove rewarding once initiated.

3. **Feedback limitation** Accurately predicting how activities will feel remains difficult from outside them—with experiential qualities often emerging through rather than existing prior to participation.

4. **Social synchronization** Group activities often generate emotional states not available individually—with shared rhythms, attention, and purpose creating experiences qualitatively different from solitary ones.

These dynamics mean waiting to participate until feeling "ready" often prevents the very experiences that would generate desired states—creating paralysis rather than protection during challenging times.

The Power of Imperfect Participation

Apocalyptic conditions often intensify the gap between idealized participation and actual capacity. Energy fluctuates. Resources become constrained. Previous standards grow increasingly unrealistic. During such periods, the concept of "imperfect participation" becomes particularly valuable—showing up however possible rather than waiting for ideal conditions.

Several participation forms prove especially accessible during difficult times:

1. **Threshold contribution** Participating at minimum viable engagement levels:

   - Showing up for brief rather than complete experiences
   - Contributing single elements to collective efforts
   - Participating remotely when in-person presence exceeds capacity
   - Engaging partially rather than comprehensively
   - Offering presence even without active contribution

2. **Authentic limitation acknowledgment** Participating while honestly naming current constraints:

   - "I can attend but may need to leave early"
   - "I'm bringing what I have, which isn't what I wish I could offer"
   - "I can participate in these aspects but not those"
   - "I'm showing up with limited capacity today"
   - "I'm here but struggling, and that's what I can bring"

3. **Companionable quiet presence** Offering witness and company without requiring active engagement:

   - Sitting with others without needing to contribute
   - Being physically present without social performance
   - Providing quiet accompaniment during activities
   - Creating background presence supporting others' engagement
   - Holding space without filling it
4. **Cyclical engagement** Participating through patterns accommodating fluctuating capacity:

   - Alternating active and passive involvement
   - Creating regular but limited contribution rhythms
   - Developing explicit on/off participation cycles
   - Establishing sustainable engagement frequencies
   - Designing participation forms matched to energy patterns

These approaches transform participation from all-or-nothing prospect to flexible engagement matched to actual circumstances—creating access to the joy that emerges through showing up without requiring impossible standards during apocalyptic times.

Overcoming Participation Barriers

Despite understanding participation's value, several common barriers often prevent engagement during difficult periods. Addressing these obstacles directly helps create access to the joy that emerges through showing up despite imperfect conditions.

1. **Perfection paralysis** The belief that participation requires meeting previous or ideal standards:

    ◦ Reframing: "Imperfect participation creates more possibility than perfect absence"
    ◦ Question: "What's the smallest viable way I could engage with this?"
    ◦ Practice: Setting explicit "good enough for now" standards matched to current capacity

- ○ Perspective: Viewing participation as process rather than performance
- ○ Support: Finding communities that welcome imperfect engagement

2. **Emotional prerequisite myths** The belief that particular feelings must precede participation:

- ○ Reframing: "Actions often create feelings rather than requiring them first"
- ○ Question: "What might become possible if I engaged despite not feeling 'ready'?"
- ○ Practice: Deliberate engagement contrary to current emotional states
- ○ Perspective: Viewing initial feelings as starting points rather than fixed conditions
- ○ Support: Communities normalizing engagement without emotional prerequisites

3. **Binary engagement thinking** The belief that participation requires complete rather than partial involvement:

- ○ Reframing: "Partial engagement creates more possibility than complete absence"

- Question: "Which specific elements feel most accessible right now?"
- Practice: Deliberately designed partial participation experiments
- Perspective: Viewing engagement as spectrum rather than binary state
- Support: Communities with graduated participation options

4. **Worthiness condition attachment** The belief that participation requires demonstrating particular value:

- Reframing: "Showing up itself creates value regardless of performance quality"
- Question: "How might my simple presence benefit this situation?"
- Practice: Noticing automatic worthiness assessments without acting on them
- Perspective: Viewing inherent rather than demonstrated value as participation basis
- Support: Communities emphasizing being over doing

Addressing these common barriers helps create access to the joy that emerges through continued engagement with life despite the very real constraints of apocalyptic times—finding aliveness not through transcending current conditions but through participating in them however imperfectly.

Tomorrow Is Another Apocalypse

Throughout this book, we've explored approaches for navigating apocalyptic times—finding meaning, connection, and yes, even joy amid conditions that might seem to preclude them. As we conclude, it's worth acknowledging a simple truth: Tomorrow is another apocalypse. The challenges continue. The difficulties remain. The work is ongoing.

This isn't pessimism but realism. Many of the crises we currently face won't resolve neatly or quickly. Climate disruption, systemic inequality, democratic erosion, technological transformation, and other major challenges will likely continue generating apocalyptic conditions for the foreseeable future.

Yet within this sobering acknowledgment lies a strange freedom. When we release expectations for swift resolution or complete transformation, space opens for sustainable engagement with ongoing reality rather than perpetual disappointment that immediate salvation hasn't arrived.

Living One Disaster at a Time

One particularly helpful approach involves what might be called "disaster unitasking"—focusing attention and response on current specific challenges rather than the entire aggregated catastrophe landscape simultaneously.

Several practices support this approach:

1. **Temporal focusing** Deliberately constraining attention to specific timeframes:

    - "Today, I'm addressing this particular challenge"
    - "This week, I'm focusing on this specific response"
    - "For the next hour, I'm attending to just this dimension"
    - "Right now, I'm dealing with what's directly in front of me"
    - "This season, I'm directing energy toward this specific area"
2. **Domain compartmentalization** Temporarily separating interconnected problems to make response manageable:

- Addressing environmental, social, and personal dimensions sequentially rather than simultaneously
- Creating designated time periods for different challenge categories
- Developing specific practices for transitions between problem domains
- Explicitly acknowledging legitimate focus limitation
- Practicing completion of current focus before shifting attention

3. **Response scaling** Matching engagement scope to actual current capacity:

- Right-sizing commitments to available resources
- Creating sustainable rhythms rather than emergency response patterns
- Developing explicit criteria for exceptional versus routine engagement
- Designing graduated response options matched to fluctuating capacity
- Normalizing appropriate scale limitation as wisdom rather than failure

4. **Milestone acknowledgment** Recognizing specific achievements within ongoing challenges:

- Celebrating particular response elements regardless of overall situation
- Creating completion markers within continuing processes
- Acknowledging effort quality independent of outcome totality
- Developing rituals for genuine completion recognition
- Finding authentic satisfaction in partial rather than only complete resolution

These approaches transform potentially overwhelming apocalyptic aggregation into manageable specific engagements—not through denial of total situation complexity but through practical focus on what can be meaningfully addressed in particular moments with available resources.

The Permission to Be Gloriously Imperfect

Perhaps the most essential element for finding joy amid ongoing apocalyptic conditions involves permission—not bestowed by external authority but granted to ourselves—to be gloriously, authentically imperfect in our response.

This permission manifests through several specific recognitions:

1. **The inevitability of limitation**
   Acknowledging fundamental constraints as universal human condition rather than personal failing:

   - Every response remains partial rather than comprehensive
   - All efforts include both success and failure elements
   - Every person faces capacity limitations regardless of commitment
   - Each choice inevitably involves both gains and losses
   - No response achieves perfection regardless of intention

2. **The value despite imperfection**
   Recognizing genuine worth in necessarily imperfect engagement:

   - Partial responses create more possibility than none
   - Imperfect efforts build capacity for subsequent attempts

- Limitation-acknowledging participation offers authentic presence
- Honest engagement with actual constraints provides real contribution
- Value emerges through process regardless of outcome perfection

3. **The freedom within constraint** Finding liberation through accepting rather than denying limitation:

- Release from impossible standards creates engagement possibility
- Honest limitation acknowledgment enables authentic connection
- Working within constraints fosters genuine creativity
- Accepting imperfection permits continuing rather than abandoning effort
- Recognizing universal limitation creates solidarity rather than isolation

4. **The humor amid difficulty** Developing capacity for lightness without minimization:

- Finding comedy in honest limitation acknowledgment
- Embracing absurdity of imperfect beings facing enormous challenges

- Allowing laughter alongside serious engagement
- Seeing humor in cosmic incongruity of our situation
- Creating joy through shared recognition of common predicament

This permission creates space for genuine joy not despite ongoing apocalyptic conditions but within them—finding aliveness, connection, and even delight in the messy, imperfect, but utterly authentic experience of being human during challenging times.

Your Invitation to the Cozy End of the World

As we conclude this book, I offer an invitation—not to denial, toxic positivity, or premature resolution, but to what might be called "the cozy end of the world." Not because ending requires coziness, but because facing difficult realities becomes more sustainable with certain qualities of heart, mind, and relationship that the concept of coziness evokes.

This invitation includes several elements:

1. **Authentic presence** Showing up fully for what's actually happening rather than what

we wish were happening:

- Seeing clearly without flinching or minimizing
- Acknowledging difficulty without magnification or reduction
- Feeling genuinely without performance or suppression
- Engaging honestly with limitation and possibility alike
- Creating relationship with reality as it exists rather than as preferred

2. **Warm connection** Developing genuine relationship amid rather than despite challenging conditions:

- Finding companionship for the journey regardless of destination
- Creating moments of authentic togetherness within larger difficulties
- Building networks of mutual care during shared challenges
- Maintaining heart connection alongside clear seeing
- Experiencing belonging regardless of circumstance resolution

3. **Gentle courage** Bringing both bravery and tenderness to apocalyptic navigation:

   - Facing reality without artificial toughness or fragility
   - Continuing engagement without either brutality or avoidance
   - Finding strength through vulnerability rather than its denial
   - Creating safety within rather than from challenge
   - Offering kindness alongside clarity in both self and other relationship

4. **Meaningful engagement** Participating in ways that generate purpose regardless of outcome:

   - Finding significance through process regardless of result
   - Creating beauty regardless of permanence
   - Offering care regardless of definitive impact
   - Developing meaning through presence rather than achievement

- Experiencing aliveness through engagement itself rather than its consequences

This cozy apocalypse orientation doesn't dismiss genuine dangers, minimize real suffering, or pretend impending systemic transformation isn't disruptive and sometimes devastating. What it offers instead is sustainable relationship with these realities—finding ways to remain fully alive, connected, and even occasionally joyful while facing rather than denying the challenging conditions of our time.

Conclusion: Your Invitation to Keep Dancing

As our journey through this book concludes, perhaps the most important thing to remember is this: The apocalypse isn't a single event but an ongoing process we're already within. The question isn't whether we'll face collapse—parts of that collapse are already underway—but how we'll live as these transformations unfold.

The approaches we've explored throughout these pages—from embracing grief to finding humor, from creating pockets of peace to building community care networks, from maintaining hope without delusion to finding joy anyway—don't offer escape from apocalyptic realities. What they offer instead is capacity to remain fully human within them.

Because that's the real invitation of the cozy apocalypse: not to transcend current conditions but to remain fully present within them, bringing all our human capacities—grief and joy, rage and tenderness, clarity and mystery, solitude and connection—to this remarkable, terrifying, beautiful moment we find ourselves navigating together.

So keep dancing, even as the music changes. Keep loving, even when outcomes remain uncertain. Keep creating beauty, even amid undeniable destruction. Keep finding moments of joy, even on difficult days. Keep showing up for life, even in your apocalypse pajamas.

Not because everything will necessarily work out fine, but because being fully alive means engaging with what is, not just what we wish would be. Not because suffering isn't real, but because joy remains possible alongside it. Not because the apocalypse isn't happening, but because we're still here to experience it—with all the responsibility and possibility that presence entails.

The world is indeed burning. And yes, your hair looks great. Both are true. Both matter. Both are part of this strange, imperfect, occasionally transcendent experience of being human during apocalyptic times.

Welcome to the cozy apocalypse. We're all in it together. Let's make it as beautiful as we can.

EPILOGUE: Tomorrow Is Another Apocalypse

And so we come to the end of this book, though not to the end of the apocalypse. Tomorrow will bring new challenges, fresh crises, unexpected difficulties. The news will continue reporting disasters. Systems will keep showing signs of strain. The future will remain stubbornly uncertain.

But you already knew that, didn't you?

You picked up this book not because you thought it would magically solve everything, but because you were looking for ways to navigate a reality you'd already recognized. You weren't seeking escape. You were seeking company for the journey.

And that's what I've tried to offer throughout these pages—not solutions that make the apocalypse disappear, but approaches that help us live with integrity, connection, and even occasional joy as we move through these challenging times together.

Living One Apocalypse at a Time

If there's one truth that stands out from all we've explored, it's the importance of living one apocalypse at a time. Not because the challenges aren't interconnected—they absolutely are—but because human attention, energy, and capacity remain finite even when problems don't.

This means:

- Focusing on today's specific difficulties rather than tomorrow's imagined catastrophes
- Addressing what's directly in front of you rather than the entire crisis landscape
- Taking care of your immediate community while staying connected to larger concerns
- Finding moments of peace amid ongoing turbulence
- Celebrating small victories without requiring complete resolution

It means recognizing that while you can't single-handedly solve climate change, democracy erosion, economic inequality, or any other systemic crisis, you can take meaningful action in your particular corner of the world today.

This isn't about ignoring the bigger picture. It's about finding sustainable ways to engage with it— ways that preserve your capacity for continued participation rather than burning you out in spectacular but short-lived bursts of heroic effort.

The Permission to Be Gloriously Imperfect

Throughout this book, we've returned repeatedly to the theme of imperfection—not as something to overcome, but as something to embrace as an inherent aspect of the human condition.

During apocalyptic times, this embracing of imperfection becomes not just psychologically healthy but practically essential. When perfect solutions remain elusive, imperfect engagement becomes the only viable option.

This means giving yourself permission to:

- Respond imperfectly to impossible situations
- Feel complicated, contradictory emotions about complex events
- Create beauty that incorporates rather than transcends limitation
- Build community through shared vulnerability rather than performed strength
- Find joy in messy, incomplete experiences rather than waiting for ideal conditions

It means recognizing that imperfection isn't a temporary state to move beyond but the fundamental condition within which all human endeavor occurs—especially during periods of significant disruption.

When we embrace this reality rather than fighting against it, we discover strange freedom. Not freedom from limitation, but freedom within it. Not perfection, but authenticity. Not transcendence, but full, messy, gloriously imperfect engagement with life as it actually is.

Your Invitation to the Cozy Apocalypse

As you close this book and continue navigating whatever apocalyptic circumstances you're facing, I offer this invitation one final time: Welcome to the cozy apocalypse.

Not because apocalypse is inherently cozy. It isn't. There's nothing cozy about climate disruption, democratic erosion, pandemic disease, economic inequality, or any other systemic crisis currently unfolding.

But coziness remains possible within apocalypse— not as escape but as resistance to forces that would reduce us to mere survival. Finding moments of warmth, connection, beauty, and joy amid difficult circumstances isn't frivolous but essential—not just for psychological wellbeing but for sustaining the very human qualities needed to face these challenges effectively.

So make your corner of the apocalypse as cozy as you can:

- Create pockets of peace amid chaos

- Build networks of mutual care
- Find moments of genuine joy without guilt
- Maintain hope without requiring certainty
- Embrace the messy middle where most of life unfolds
- Show up imperfectly but authentically for what matters most

Do this not because it will necessarily change the larger trajectory of current crises, but because it changes how you experience navigating them—and how those around you experience your presence within shared challenges.

Beyond Self-Help: The Bigger Picture

While much of this book has focused on individual and small community approaches to apocalyptic times, I want to emphasize once more that systemic problems ultimately require systemic responses. Personal resilience matters, but it cannot substitute for collective action addressing root causes rather than just symptoms.

The practices we've explored—from grief processing to collective care networks, from hope without delusion to finding joy anyway—don't replace political engagement, system redesign, or structural transformation. They sustain us through the long, difficult work of pursuing these larger changes.

In this sense, personal apocalypse navigation practices serve not as alternatives to systemic change but as essential foundations for it— preserving the capacity for sustained engagement rather than rapid burnout, for strategic persistence rather than reactive despair.

So as you implement approaches from this book in your personal life, keep asking the bigger questions:

- What systems need transformation rather than just individual adaptation?
- Where might collective action address root causes rather than just managing symptoms?
- How can personal practices support rather than substitute for structural change?
- What larger movements might your individual efforts connect with and support?
- How might personal resilience translate into political effectiveness?

These questions don't have simple answers, but asking them keeps our individual responses connected to the larger context within which they occur—preventing personal practice from becoming just another form of privileged withdrawal from collective challenges.

A Final Word of Gratitude

Before closing, I want to offer sincere gratitude to you, the reader, for engaging with these difficult topics. It would be easier to look away—to distract yourself with endless entertainment, numb yourself with various substances, or pretend everything is fine when it clearly isn't.

The fact that you've chosen engagement over avoidance matters. It represents a fundamental moral choice to remain present to reality as it is rather than retreating into comfortable delusion. That choice deserves recognition and respect.

Whatever specific approaches from this book prove helpful in your particular circumstances, please remember this: Your continued engagement with challenging realities—your choice to face them with clarity, compassion, and courage rather than turning away—represents something profound and worthy, regardless of specific outcomes.

As Rebecca Solnit writes: "Hope is not a lottery ticket you can sit on the sofa and clutch, feeling lucky... Hope is an ax you break down doors with in an emergency."

Thank you for picking up the ax. Thank you for staying engaged. Thank you for bringing your unique gifts to this remarkable, terrifying, beautiful moment we find ourselves navigating together.

The world is indeed burning. And we're still here, finding ways to create meaning, connection, and occasionally even joy amid the flames. Both realities matter. Both deserve acknowledgment. Both are part of the complex truth of being human during apocalyptic times.

Tomorrow is another apocalypse. And we'll face it together, one day at a time, as best we imperfectly can.

Welcome to the cozy apocalypse. Let's make it as beautiful as we possibly can.

APPENDIX

Apocalypse Playlist: Songs for the End of the World

Music provides one of our most powerful tools for processing complex emotions, finding connection, and creating moments of joy even during difficult times. This playlist offers songs across genres that resonate specifically with apocalyptic experiences —not as escape but as companions for the journey.

For Processing Grief

- "It's Quiet Uptown" - Lin-Manuel Miranda (Hamilton)
- "Tears in Heaven" - Eric Clapton
- "The Background World" - Nine Inch Nails
- "Kettering" - The Antlers
- "Motion Picture Soundtrack" - Radiohead
- "The Drugs Don't Work" - The Verve
- "Re: Stacks" - Bon Iver
- "Landslide" - Fleetwood Mac
- "Breathe Me" - Sia
- "Casimir Pulaski Day" - Sufjan Stevens

For Finding Courage

- "Uprising" - Muse
- "Wake Up" - Rage Against the Machine
- "Titanium" - David Guetta ft. Sia
- "Rise Up" - Andra Day
- "Brave" - Sara Bareilles
- "Freedom" - Beyoncé ft. Kendrick Lamar
- "Fight Song" - Rachel Platten
- "Survivor" - Destiny's Child
- "Roar" - Katy Perry
- "This Is Me" - Keala Settle (The Greatest Showman)

For Embracing Complexity

- "Both Sides, Now" - Joni Mitchell
- "Shake It Out" - Florence + The Machine
- "Rainbow" - Kacey Musgraves
- "What A Wonderful World" - Louis Armstrong
- "Ooh La La" - Faces
- "Hand In My Pocket" - Alanis Morissette
- "The Middle" - Jimmy Eat World
- "Changes" - David Bowie
- "Everything Now" - Arcade Fire
- "Little Talks" - Of Monsters and Men

For Apocalyptic Times Specifically

- "It's The End Of The World As We Know It (And I Feel Fine)" - R.E.M.

- "The Future" - Leonard Cohen
- "We Didn't Start the Fire" - Billy Joel
- "Sign of the Times" - Harry Styles
- "Wasteland, Baby!" - Hozier
- "Eve of Destruction" - Barry McGuire
- "Idioteque" - Radiohead
- "99 Red Balloons" - Nena
- "Don't Fear The Reaper" - Blue Öyster Cult
- "Bad Moon Rising" - Creedence Clearwater Revival

For Finding Joy Anyway

- "This Year" - The Mountain Goats
- "Float On" - Modest Mouse
- "Three Little Birds" - Bob Marley & The Wailers
- "Good As Hell" - Lizzo
- "Don't Stop Me Now" - Queen
- "Walking on Sunshine" - Katrina & The Waves
- "Dancing Queen" - ABBA
- "Happy" - Pharrell Williams
- "I Will Survive" - Gloria Gaynor
- "Resilient" - Rising Appalachia

For Collective Resistance

- "Get Up Stand Up" - Bob Marley & The Wailers

- "Fight the Power" - Public Enemy
- "Killing in the Name" - Rage Against the Machine
- "Alright" - Kendrick Lamar
- "People Have the Power" - Patti Smith
- "Freedom" - Beyoncé ft. Kendrick Lamar
- "This Is America" - Childish Gambino
- "Revolution" - The Beatles
- "The Times They Are a-Changin'" - Bob Dylan
- "For What It's Worth" - Buffalo Springfield

Emergency Contacts: Resources for When It All Gets Too Much

While this book offers many approaches for navigating apocalyptic times, there are moments when professional support becomes essential. These resources provide immediate assistance during acute crisis as well as ongoing support for longer-term challenges.

Crisis Resources (United States)

- **988 Suicide & Crisis Lifeline**: Call or text 988 (Available 24/7)
- **Crisis Text Line**: Text HOME to 741741 (Available 24/7)

- **Trevor Project** (LGBTQ+ youth): 1-866-488-7386 or text START to 678678
- **Veterans Crisis Line**: 1-800-273-8255 and Press 1
- **Trans Lifeline**: 1-877-565-8860
- **National Sexual Assault Hotline**: 1-800-656-HOPE (4673)
- **National Domestic Violence Hotline**: 1-800-799-7233 or text START to 88788
- **Disaster Distress Helpline**: 1-800-985-5990 or text TalkWithUs to 66746

Crisis Resources (International)

- **International Association for Suicide Prevention**: https://www.iasp.info/resources/Crisis_Centres/ (Directory of crisis centers worldwide)
- **Befrienders Worldwide**: https://www.befrienders.org/ (Volunteer emotional support helplines globally)

Finding Ongoing Mental Health Support

- **Psychology Today Therapist Finder**: https://www.psychologytoday.com/us/therapists
- **Open Path Collective**: https://openpathcollective.org/ (Affordable therapy options)

- **Therapy for Black Girls Directory**: https://providers.therapyforblackgirls.com/
- **National Queer and Trans Therapists of Color Network**: https://www.nqttcn.com/
- **Anxiety and Depression Association of America**: https://adaa.org/finding-help
- **Latinx Therapy Directory**: https://latinxtherapy.com/find-a-therapist/

Mutual Aid Resources

- **Mutual Aid Hub**: https://www.mutualaidhub.org/
- **Big Door Brigade**: http://bigdoorbrigade.com/what-is-mutual-aid/
- **Mutual Aid Disaster Relief**: https://mutualaiddisasterrelief.org/

Grief Support Resources

- **The Dinner Party**: https://www.thedinnerparty.org/ (Community for those who have experienced significant loss)
- **Modern Loss**: https://modernloss.com/ (Community, resources, and support for grief)
- **The Grief Recovery Method**: https://www.griefrecoverymethod.com/
- **Refuge in Grief**: https://refugeingrief.com/

Climate Anxiety Resources

- **Climate Psychology Alliance**: https://www.climatepsychologyalliance.org/
- **The Good Grief Network**: https://www.goodgriefnetwork.org/
- **All We Can Save Project**: https://www.allwecansave.earth/ (Climate community-building)

Cozy Apocalypse Recipes: Comfort Food for Uncomfortable Times

Food nourishes not just our bodies but our spirits, especially during difficult times. These recipes focus on:

1. Simple ingredients that remain relatively accessible
2. Flexible approaches allowing substitution based on what's available
3. Comfort that sustains both physically and emotionally
4. Options for batch cooking when energy is limited

Apocalypse Pantry Pasta

Ingredients:

- 1 pound pasta (any shape)
- 2-4 tablespoons olive oil (or any cooking oil)
- 4-6 garlic cloves, minced (or 1-2 teaspoons garlic powder)
- 1 can (14 oz) diced tomatoes

- 1 can (14 oz) beans (chickpeas, white beans, or whatever you have)
- Salt and pepper to taste
- Optional add-ins (use what you have): canned tuna, frozen vegetables, herbs, red pepper flakes, parmesan cheese

Instructions:

1. Boil pasta in salted water according to package directions.
2. While pasta cooks, heat oil in a large pan over medium heat.
3. Add garlic and cook until fragrant, about 30 seconds.
4. Add tomatoes (with juice) and beans (drained), bring to simmer.
5. Season with salt, pepper, and any optional seasonings.
6. Drain pasta, reserving ½ cup cooking water.
7. Add pasta to sauce along with any optional add-ins.
8. If needed, add reserved pasta water to reach desired consistency.
9. Stir to combine and serve.

Flexible Comfort Soup

Ingredients:

- 2 tablespoons oil or butter
- 1 onion, diced (or 1 tablespoon onion powder)
- 2-3 carrots, diced (or any vegetables you have)
- 2-3 celery stalks, diced (or any vegetables you have)
- 2 cloves garlic, minced (or 1 teaspoon garlic powder)
- 6 cups broth (vegetable, chicken, or even water with bouillon)
- 1 can (14 oz) diced tomatoes (optional)
- 1-2 cups dried lentils, rice, or small pasta
- 1 can (14 oz) beans, drained
- Salt, pepper, herbs to taste
- Optional: handful of greens, squeeze of lemon, parmesan

Instructions:

1. Heat oil in large pot over medium heat.
2. Add onion, carrots, celery (or substitute vegetables); cook until softened, about 5 minutes.
3. Add garlic, cook 30 seconds until fragrant.
4. Add broth, tomatoes if using, and lentils/rice/pasta.

5. Bring to boil, then reduce to simmer until grain is cooked (20-40 minutes depending on what you're using).
6. Add beans and any greens, simmer 5 more minutes.
7. Season to taste with salt, pepper, herbs.
8. Finish with lemon juice or parmesan if available.

Emergency Comfort Cookies

Ingredients:

- 1 cup nut or seed butter (peanut, almond, sunflower)
- 3/4 cup sugar (white or brown)
- 1 egg (or 1/4 cup applesauce or mashed banana)
- 1/2 teaspoon baking soda
- 1/4 teaspoon salt
- Optional add-ins: chocolate chips, dried fruit, nuts, seeds

Instructions:

1. Preheat oven to 350°F (175°C).
2. Mix all ingredients together in a bowl until well combined.
3. Form into approximately 12 balls and place on baking sheet.

4. Flatten slightly with fork.
5. Bake 10-12 minutes until edges are golden.
6. Cool on sheet for 5 minutes before transferring to rack.

One-Pot Rice & Bean Comfort Bowl

Ingredients:

- 2 tablespoons oil
- 1 onion, diced (or 1 tablespoon onion powder)
- 2-3 cloves garlic, minced (or 1 teaspoon garlic powder)
- 1 cup rice (any type)
- 1 can (14 oz) beans, drained
- 2 cups water or broth
- 1 teaspoon each: cumin, paprika (or any available spices)
- Salt and pepper to taste
- Optional toppings: avocado, salsa, cheese, hot sauce, lime

Instructions:

1. Heat oil in pot with lid over medium heat.
2. Add onion, cook until softened, about 5 minutes.

3. Add garlic and spices, cook 30 seconds until fragrant.
4. Add rice, stir to coat with oil and spices.
5. Add beans and liquid, bring to boil.
6. Reduce heat to low, cover, and simmer until rice is tender and liquid absorbed (about 15-20 minutes).
7. Let stand covered 5 minutes after cooking.
8. Fluff with fork and add optional toppings.

No-Knead Apocalypse Bread

Ingredients:

- 3 cups all-purpose flour (can substitute up to 1 cup with whole wheat)
- 1 1/2 teaspoons salt
- 1/2 teaspoon instant yeast
- 1 1/2 cups water, room temperature

Instructions:

1. In large bowl, mix flour, salt and yeast.
2. Add water and stir until blended (dough will be shaggy).
3. Cover bowl with plastic wrap or towel and let rest 12-18 hours at room temperature.
4. When surface is dotted with bubbles, dough is ready.

5. Place dough on floured surface, sprinkle with flour and fold over a few times.
6. Let rest 15 minutes.
7. Shape into ball, place on floured surface, cover and let rise 1-2 hours until doubled.
8. 30 minutes before dough is ready, preheat oven to 450°F with heavy covered pot inside (Dutch oven, ceramic, Pyrex).
9. When pot is hot, carefully place dough inside.
10. Cover with lid and bake 30 minutes.
11. Remove lid and bake another 15-30 minutes until browned.
12. Cool completely before slicing.

Building Your Personalized Apocalypse Toolkit

Throughout this book, we've explored many approaches for navigating apocalyptic times. This section helps you create a personalized toolkit drawing on practices most relevant to your specific circumstances.

Step 1: Assess Your Current Challenges

Take a few minutes to identify which aspects of apocalyptic times most significantly impact your wellbeing:

Environmental Impacts:

- Climate anxiety
- Direct effects from extreme weather
- Environmentally-triggered health issues
- Resource limitations or disruptions

Social/Political Challenges:

- Political polarization in relationships
- Democracy concerns
- Rights/safety for your identity groups
- Community breakdown

- Information overwhelm/misinformation

Economic Factors:

- Financial precarity
- Housing insecurity
- Job instability
- Resource scarcity
- Economic inequality impacts

Health Dimensions:

- Pandemic effects (direct or indirect)
- Healthcare access issues
- Mental health impacts
- Chronic condition management amid system strain
- Caregiver responsibilities

Existential Aspects:

- Purpose/meaning questions
- Future uncertainty
- Legacy concerns
- Spiritual/religious framework disruption
- Mortality awareness

Step 2: Identify Your Available Resources

Take inventory of resources currently available to support your resilience:

Internal Resources:

- Skills and knowledge
- Personal practices that help regulate emotions
- Creative outlets
- Spiritual or meaning frameworks
- Past experience navigating difficulty

Relationship Resources:

- Supportive individuals
- Communities (formal or informal)
- Professional support networks
- Online connections
- Animal companions

Material Resources:

- Stable housing (permanent or temporary)
- Financial reserves or income
- Food security
- Access to transportation
- Digital connectivity

Time/Energy Resources:

- Available time for self-care
- Energy levels and patterns
- Attention capacity
- Schedule flexibility
- Cognitive bandwidth

Environmental Resources:

- Access to nature
- Safe outdoor spaces
- Comfortable indoor environments
- Quiet or low-stimulation options
- Beauty access (natural or created)

Step 3: Design Your Personalized Toolkit

Based on your specific challenges and available resources, select practices from different categories that best match your current circumstances:

For Emotional Processing:

- Grief rituals (Chapter 1)
- Validation practices (Chapter 1)
- Humor approaches (Chapter 9)
- Joy cultivation (Chapter 8)
- Complexity holding (Chapter 15)

For Mental Wellbeing:

- Information management (Chapter 11)
- Cognitive load reduction (Chapter 11)
- The "Fuck It" Bucket System (Chapter 11)
- Hope frameworks (Chapter 14)
- Catastrophe aesthetics (Chapter 15)

For Physical Support:

- Micro-routines (Chapter 6)
- Emergency reset protocol (Chapter 11)
- Comfort recipes (Appendix)
- Sensory grounding practices (Chapter 4)
- Extremely boring habits (Chapter 6)

For Social Connection:

- Apocalypse crew development (Chapter 5)
- Micro-community building (Chapter 13)
- Capacity-based contribution (Chapter 13)
- Communication templates (Chapter 11)
- Imperfect participation approaches (Chapter 15)

For Meaning/Purpose:

- Micro-thriving practices (Chapter 10)
- Creative approaches (Chapter 12)
- Five-minute wins (Chapter 10)

- Imperfect participation (Chapter 15)
- Tree-planting perspectives (Chapter 14)

Step 4: Create Implementation Structures

Develop simple structures to integrate selected practices into daily life:

Morning Micro-Ritual: Select 1-3 brief practices that help set intention and connection for the day.

Emergency Response Plan: Identify specific practices for acute overwhelm or crisis moments.

Daily Anchors: Connect practices to existing daily activities to build sustainable habits.

Weekly Review: Schedule brief assessment of which practices are helping and which need adjustment.

Support Activation Protocol: Create clear steps for accessing support when individual practices aren't sufficient.

Seasonal Adjustment Framework: Plan for modifying practices based on seasonal energy and capacity fluctuation.

Step 5: Remember Implementation Principles

As you implement your personalized toolkit, keep these principles in mind:

1. **Start extremely small** - Begin with tiny, consistent practices rather than ambitious regimens
2. **Prioritize sustainability** over immediate impact
3. **Expect adaptation needs** as circumstances change
4. **Mix both preventive and responsive approaches**
5. **Include joy alongside functionality**
6. **Embrace imperfect implementation**
7. **Create both individual and collective components**
8. **Maintain flexibility rather than rigidity**
9. **Recognize tool limitations** for structural problems
10. **Celebrate genuine effort regardless of outcome**

Remember that your apocalypse toolkit isn't about achieving perfect resilience but supporting genuine engagement with life as it actually is—with all its challenges, possibilities, beauty, and difficulty. The goal isn't transcending apocalyptic conditions but finding ways to remain fully human within them.

Welcome to the cozy apocalypse. You're now equipped to make it as beautiful as you possibly can.

ACKNOWLEDGMENTS

This book exists because of countless conversations with friends, family, colleagues, and sometimes perfect strangers about how to navigate these apocalyptic times without losing our minds or our humanity. Thank you to everyone who shared their stories, strategies, breakdowns, and breakthroughs with me.

Special thanks to:

My children

The researchers, activists, artists, and thinkers whose work informed these pages—especially those developing frameworks for collective resilience and justice during these challenging times.

My apocalypse crew. Your friendship, wisdom, and willingness to both laugh and cry with me through all of this has been my greatest source of resilience.

My parents, who taught me that difficult times require both clear-eyed realism and unrelenting hope.

And finally, to you, the reader. Thank you for picking up this book, for staying engaged with our messy reality, and for doing your best to create moments of beauty amid the chaos. Your continued presence matters more than you know.

ABOUT THE AUTHOR

QR McKinsey is a writer and advocate for what she calls "practical liberation"—the unglamorous but essential work of freeing ourselves from systems that don't serve us, one strategic half-ass at a time.

Her journey to becoming the voice behind the Half-Ass Revolution began not with a grand epiphany but with a complete breakdown in the Target paper goods aisle. After spending fifteen minutes comparing the per-sheet price of various paper towel brands while simultaneously mediating a sibling dispute, responding to work emails, and trying to remember if they needed milk, she had what she now refers to as her "enough moment."

Her previous books in the Half-Ass Revolution series include "The Joy of Missing Out: A Field Guide to Strategic Absence," "The Emergency Fund That Isn't Your Change Jar: Financial Half-Assery for Single Moms," and "The Silent Scream: Surviving Parenthood Without Losing Your Mind."

DISCUSSION GUIDE

For Book Clubs & Community Groups

1. Which part of navigating apocalyptic times do you find most challenging: acknowledging reality, maintaining hope, finding joy, or something else entirely?

2. In Chapter 1, the author suggests that accepting how bad things are can actually help us feel better. Have you experienced this paradox in your own life?

3. Chapter 5 explores the concept of an "apocalypse crew." Who makes up your crew, and what qualities make someone particularly valuable during difficult times?

4. The book distinguishes between toxic positivity and genuine joy amid difficulty. How do you recognize the difference in your own

life or in messages you encounter?

5. In Chapter 10, the author introduces the concept of "micro-thriving." What are some five-minute wins that have made a difference in your own navigation of challenging times?

6. Chapter 12 suggests that creativity becomes more essential, not less, during crisis. Has creative expression helped you process difficult experiences? In what ways?

7. The concept of "hope without delusion" in Chapter 14 proposes a middle path between blind optimism and fatalistic despair. Where do you currently find yourself on this spectrum?

8. The epilogue suggests we approach the apocalypse "one day at a time." How might this approach change your relationship to seemingly overwhelming challenges?

9. Which practical tool or concept from the book resonated most strongly with you, and why?

10. If you were to add a chapter to this book based on your own experience, what would it be called and what would it explore?

RESOURCES FOR FURTHER EXPLORATION

Books

- *A Paradise Built in Hell* by Rebecca Solnit
- *Hope in the Dark* by Rebecca Solnit
- *Emergent Strategy* by adrienne maree brown
- *Pleasure Activism* by adrienne maree brown
- *Braiding Sweetgrass* by Robin Wall Kimmerer
- *Man's Search for Meaning* by Viktor E. Frankl
- *The Mushroom at the End of the World* by Anna Lowenhaupt Tsing
- *Learning to Die in the Anthropocene* by Roy Scranton
- *The World We Need* edited by Audrea Lim
- *All We Can Save* edited by Ayana Elizabeth Johnson and Katharine K. Wilkinson

Organizations

- The Good Grief Network (goodgriefnetwork.org)
- Transition Network (transitionnetwork.org)
- Mutual Aid Disaster Relief (mutualaiddisasterrelief.org)
- The All We Can Save Project (allwecansave.earth)
- Post Carbon Institute (postcarbon.org)
- The Work That Reconnects Network (workthatreconnects.org)

Podcasts

- "How to Survive the End of the World" with adrienne maree brown and Autumn Brown
- "For the Wild" with Ayana Young
- "Facing It" with Dr. Jennifer Atkinson
- "The Resilient" with Sasha Dingle
- "Mothers of Invention" with Mary Robinson and Maeve Higgins
- "Outrage and Optimism" with Christiana Figueres

Online Communities

- The Resilience Building Network (resilience.org)
- Transition US (transitionus.org/community)

- Climate Psychology Alliance (climatepsychologyalliance.org)
- Wiser.org (online directory for sustainability and social justice groups)

Courses & Workshops

- The Work That Reconnects (workshops based on Joanna Macy's work)
- The Good Grief Network's "10-Steps to Personal Resilience & Empowerment in a Chaotic Climate"
- Climate Psychology Alliance training programs
- Transition Towns movement training
- Post Carbon Institute's "Think Resilience" course

Remember: No book or resource can provide all the answers, but together they can help us develop more nuanced and sustainable approaches to navigating apocalyptic times. Always balance individual practices with collective action addressing root causes of current crises.

www.ingramcontent.com/pod-product-compliance
Lightning Source LLC
Chambersburg PA
CBHW061545120626
46550CB00004B/1376